Mining Town

The Photographic Record of T.N. Barnard and Nellie Stockbridge from the Coeur d'Alenes

MINING TOWN

The Photographic Record of
T.N. Barnard and Nellie Stockbridge
from the Coeur d'Alenes

by Patricia Hart and Ivar Nelson

UNIVERSITY OF WASHINGTON PRESS

Seattle and London

IDAHO STATE HISTORICAL SOCIETY

Boise

To Katrina and her grandparents,
Ruth Hart, Carroll and Genevieve Nelson

Book design by Dana Sloan

Library of Congress Cataloging in Publication Data
will be found at the back of this book.

ISBN: 0-295-96105-8

Printed in the United States of America

PREFACE

None of our research prepared us for the sight of miners working miles underground—drilling with noisy, clumsy machines; crawling up narrow, timber-framed passageways; dumping blasted-out ore and rock down wooden chutes to ore cars below. The work is hot, demanding, and dangerous. Often wet and always oppressive, it is the kind of work that wears the body down.

Our own underground experience took place two miles in and one mile down—at the bottom of the Star Mine, operated by Hecla Mining Company near Burke in the Coeur d'Alene mining district of northern Idaho. It left us covered with rock dust, mud, and sweat. It also left us with the realization that modern technology has not entirely freed hard-rock miners from the drudgery and danger that so characterized the early days of mining underground. There still remains tension between miners and their work, between miners and management, and among miners themselves—tension that gave the frontier mining towns of the Coeur d'Alenes their unique character. Life and livelihoods were insecure; emotions ran high and were expressed in direct fashion. This much has not changed.

The transition of frontier individualists to laborers and small-town citizens is part of a story that took place throughout the western United States at the turn of the century as the industrial revolution, economic centralization, and political nationalism transformed American life. As we studied the magnificent Barnard–Stockbridge photograph collection at the University of Idaho, we saw a challenging opportunity to examine early mining history and small-town life in light of these national trends.

The Barnard-Stockbridge collection is a wealth of such historical information because it comprises the work of a single studio, located at the commercial center of one of the richest mining areas of the world, and because it may be the most complete, unbroken visual record of a mining district in existence, covering nearly eighty years of mining and town history. Together the negatives and prints provide a chronicle of small changes—a microcosm of the transformation that swept the United States at the turn of the century.

In selecting photographs for this book, we looked for both historical significance and quality of image. Because the most pronounced social changes took place in the Coeur d'Alenes between the time T. N. Barnard arrived in the area in the late 1880s and World War I, we chose nearly all of the photographs from that period. We are fortunate that, with few exceptions, the negatives are well-processed and well-preserved gelatin dry-plate glass negatives, which have the characteristic lifelike clarity of that medium.

We examined each photograph from two perspectives. First, we tried to identify each person and object in the photograph and rebuild the scene. Second, we placed each picture in its historical context and searched for relationships between life in the Coeur d'Alenes and contemporary national trends. Pursuing details of each photograph required work with newspapers, property deeds, street directories, and personal interviews with descendants and participants. The story of each photograph was developed on its own, then placed in the more general historical setting.

We have two goals with this approach: to use these photographs as historic documents to tell significant parts of the Coeur d'Alene story, and to present in all their clarity some of the best and some of the most interesting images of these two pioneer photographers.

The history of the Barnard Studio—from the beginning when young Thomas Nathan Barnard arrived in the boom town of Murray, Idaho, to Nellie Stockbridge's death in 1965—is told in the first chapter. The story of the collection—from its donation to the University of Idaho by Stockbridge's heirs to the completion of the monumental task of sorting and cataloging—is related for photohistorians and other interested persons at the end of this book.

Patricia Hart
Ivar Nelson
Moscow, Idaho
June, 1984

ACKNOWLEDGMENTS

This book acknowledges the work of two photographers for whose sense of the historic present we are grateful; and though we did not have the privilege of meeting T. N. Barnard or Nellie Stockbridge, we have had the pleasure of knowing them through their families. We are indebted to the gracious cooperation and enthusiasm of Ruth Ray of Oklahoma City, niece of Stockbridge; and for their insights we thank another niece, Helen Henrickson of Tualatin, Oregon, and grand-nephew Fred Stockbridge of Anderson, California.

On Barnard's side, T. N.'s great-granddaughter, Cirrelda B. Mills of Boulder, Colorado provided many family documents and encouragement. Mrs. William Barnard of Spokane, Washington, wife of the late son of the photographer, generously donated items of family history to supplement the collection at the University of Idaho Library.

Many individuals have contributed to the preservation of this magnificent collection. Stockbridge's heirs set things in motion by donating the collection to the University of Idaho. Richard Magnuson and Henry Day of Wallace recognized the significance of the studio material and helped bring the collection to the university. The curatorial skill of Charles Webbert, former head of University of Idaho Special Collections, laid the groundwork for the use of the collection. The meticulous and resourceful cataloging carried out under his direction by Lois Ackaret and Donna Smith has opened to the public a window on the historic Coeur d'Alene district, and for their assistance in writing this book, we are indeed grateful.

Many people in Wallace and elsewhere have helped us in our search—among them children and grandchildren of pioneer families; newcomers with a lively interest in the district's past; and often individuals whose knowledge of the events pictured in this book comes from having been there themselves. They have been an essential link to our research of the region's past.

Source material for *Mining Town* is scattered among state and county historical societies, libraries, and archives. At each of these sources there is at least one individual who patiently searched along with us for a missing fact or a thread to a story. We hope they will recognize a faithful rendering of their contribution in this text.

The idea for a book on the collection started with former University of Idaho librarian, Milo Nelson; and former University of Washington Press editor Bruce Wilcox nursed it through its nascent stages, with much penetrating advice and urging on. Several individuals read the book in manuscript, each making significant contributions to its final form. To that end we particularly wish to thank Judy Austin and Merle Wells of the Idaho State Historical Society, Phil Lindstrom of Wallace, and Diana Armstrong of Moscow, Idaho.

Finally, we wish to thank Bill Woolston, who printed the fragile photographic negatives for the publication of this book.

CONTENTS

Introduction / *ix*

The Barnard Studio / *1*

Gold Mining / *15*

Silver Mining / *27*

Mining Wars / *49*

Town Beginnings / *71*

Isolation / 79

Local Entrepreneurs / *99*

A Settled Community / *117*

National Pride, Local Vice / *131*

Studio Photography / *147*

The Collection / *159*

Select Bibliography / *163*

Map / *170*

List of Plates / *173*

INTRODUCTION

The valleys are narrow, some so deep that sun strikes their streambeds only at midday, even in the summer. During the winters that last from October to April, snow piles up on the steep slopes stopped from avalanche by thick evergreen forests. When the snow melts, the normally clear mountain streams turn muddy as they rush to valley floors, uprooting trees and rolling boulders down their constricted paths.

The wilderness of northern Idaho was often impassable. After a treacherous autumn and winter of 1853 spent pushing through a military wagon road between the Missouri and Columbia rivers, Lieutenant John Mullan conceded that his proposed route through the Coeur d'Alenes was too snowy and steep to be a suitable route for a transcontinental railroad. The only flat areas were cedar swamps. The few passes that existed were blocked much of the year. There was an easier route to the north, and no doubt the Mullan road would have been reclaimed by natural forces had it not been for the discovery of gold at Prichard Creek on the North Fork of the Coeur d'Alene River in 1883.

First gold, then silver, led thousands of prospectors and miners to the Coeur d'Alenes in the last two decades of the nineteenth century. While placer gold in streambeds provided the impetus for the stampede in the winter of '83–84, no major gold veins worth long-term development were ever discovered. Silver proved far more profitable. Large deposits of silver-bearing tetrahedrite ore have been continuously mined for one hundred years, making the Coeur d'Alenes one of the most successful silver-mining areas of the world. Less glamorous but more lucrative has been the mining of lead and zinc sulfides, which sophisticated mining technologies have made profitable products of the district.

These ores are mined underground, in tunnels and shafts that follow veins for miles under the surface. This is hard-rock mining, blasting through quartzite and granite to get at the ore, which is then lifted aboveground and transported to mills. The labor underground requires special skills—skills that set the miners apart from other workers on the western frontier.

The early miners were well paid by frontier standards, but not well enough to compensate for their long, dangerous, and debilitating work. After the gold rush had ebbed and the silver mines were established, these men of many nationalities and their families became the permanent population of the Coeur d'Alenes. Prospectors and frontier romantics moved on, but hard-rock miners stayed to work for—and fight against—the entrepreneurial capitalists who owned the mines at that time.

The work underground was harsh, and so were the battles between capital and labor for control of the district. After nine years of skirmishes and two major battles, capital won, with the support of state and federal troops. The unions have never again been as powerful as they were in the turbulent days of the last decade of the nineteenth century.

Due to a mining heritage and geographic isolation, the frontier spirit lived on in the Coeur d'Alenes: Wallace was decidedly wet during Prohibition, maintained a thriving red-light district in puritanical, Mormon-influenced Idaho, and has long stood out as a Democratic island in a sea of Idaho Republicanism. This book tells, in part, the story of a distinct regional character and its survival in face of amalgamating national trends at the dawn of the twentieth century.

THE BARNARD STUDIO

IT TOOK a certain audacious innocence for a nineteen-year-old on his first trip away from home to leave the settled frontier of the Midwest in 1881 and come to the unsettled frontier of Montana. Thomas Nathan Barnard was a happy young man just out of high school with many friends and a close-knit family. Yet there is no indication that Nate, as he was called by his family and friends, ever looked back to the well-ordered streets of Waukon, the northeastern Iowa town where he grew up.

Nate Barnard went first to Miles City in eastern Montana, where he apprenticed himself to another Waukon emigrant, Laton Alton Huffman. By working for Huffman at his studio Barnard became involved in a rich photographic tradition. Huffman had learned photography from his father, Perrin Cuppy Huffman, proprietor of a studio in Waukon. In the summer of 1878, Laton Huffman went north to Moorhead, Minnesota, where he worked for Frank Jay Haynes. Haynes, then roving the northern frontier, was soon to become the official photographer of the Northern Pacific Railroad. Haynes liked Huffman, whom he invited to live at the studio. They discovered a shared vision of the vanishing frontier, and both were anxious to get out and photograph the

West of their dreams before it disappeared. Huffman moved on to Montana, where he became post photographer at Fort Keogh before moving into nearby Miles City and establishing a studio.

Miles City was a crude, rough-timbered town of the Great Plains, swept in the summer by hot, dusty prairie winds and in the winter by bitter, drifting blizzards. Just five years earlier, Custer had died at Little Big Horn south of Miles City. Cheyenne and Crow Indians wandered in and out of town, living on the fringes of white society. A military post turned cattle town, Miles City thrived on the commerce of ranchers, farmers, drinkers, card players, and prostitutes. This is where Barnard met up with Huffman in 1881.

Barnard worked for Huffman as a photographic printer and general assistant for two years. He lived with Huffman at the studio, printed Huffman's work, and learned to take photographs himself. Huffman was becoming well known for his pictures, and Barnard was learning the trade. He was doing so just as the western frontier was running out of room, when the role of the itinerant western photographer was disappearing along with the frontier way of life. The railroad reached Miles City in September, 1881, and Laton Huffman later said: "There was no frontier after the railroad."

Both Haynes and Huffman were by then established photographers of that era and place. Haynes was practicing his trade along the Northern Pacific line and taking magnificent pictures of the Yellowstone country. He built his later career on the photographic concession in Yellowstone National Park.

Huffman specialized in photography of the open range, capturing the demise of the large buffalo herds, the beginning of reservation life, and the coming of cattle ranching to Montana. His interest lay in Indian life, forts, cavalry, bison hunts, panoramics, and townscapes. He published

------

(Overleaf) BARNARD WITH CIGAR (N.D.).
Clothed in a three-piece suit and smoking a cigar, Barnard looks every inch the mining entrepreneur in this studio portrait taken early in the twentieth century.

catalogs of his work, selling primarily to easterners curious about the exotic West. Most of Huffman's landscape photographs became stereographs — an image that had to be viewed through a stereoscopic viewer to be properly appreciated. In addition to stereographs, full-size (usually 5x8) pictures mounted on cards inscribed with the photographer's imprint were popular. There was also a growing market for souvenir postcards. Unlike portraits, which were done on commission, stereographs, full-size prints, and postcards were done on speculation. To make a profit, many prints from a single negative had to be sold. This required marketing the prints; thus, the photographer as publisher was born.

The frontier landscape photographer was a prospector with his camera, taking a picture in hopes that it would strike the public's fancy. A negative of proven popularity was kept and used for many years, part of the photographer's "working file." Huffman introduced Barnard to landscape photography as it was being practiced on the western frontier in the 1880s. As Huffman's apprentice, Barnard was trained to keep an eye out for the marketable picture.

In 1881, Huffman was starting to experiment with the revolutionary gelatin dry-plate negatives, one of the first photographers in the West to do so. The wet-plate glass negative then in common use required a great deal of time and effort to sensitize, expose, and develop. Dry-plate negatives, at first more expensive, were sensitized in the manufacturing process, could be stored, and once exposed did not have to be developed immediately. Although Barnard was trained in both techniques at Huffman's studio, he used dry plates when he began work in the Coeur d'Alenes because they had become cheaper.

By the summer of 1883, Barnard was ready to move further west, but he was looking for land, not photographic opportunities. He may have taken one of the first trains of the Northern Pacific Railroad's newly completed transcontinental line, because it was just one month after the line was completed in September, 1883, that he filed a claim on 160 acres of homestead near Prosser, on the Yakima River

in Washington Territory. Winter was no time to work the land, and Barnard went to Pendleton, Oregon, taking a job in a dry-goods store until the following July.

Barnard turned out to be more a frontier romantic than a pioneer farmer. For whatever reason, he did not "prove up" his homestead, and by the fall of 1885 he had traveled back to Miles City, probably taking the Northern Pacific through Thompson Falls, Montana, a taking-off point for gold hunters heading for the Coeur d'Alenes in Idaho Territory. The excitement of the rush might have had some impact on Barnard, because in August of 1886 he bought a camera from Huffman for $88.50 ($50 down and the rest on credit) and was on his way to the goldfields on the North Fork of the Coeur d'Alene River.

Murray, called Murrayville when F. Jay Haynes took the first recorded photographs of it in 1884, was a slightly faded frontier boom town of rough-sawn lumber and muddy, rutted streets when Barnard established his first photographic studio there in a log cabin on a hillside above the town. He was not the first to do photographic business there—a man named Allison advertised his picture-taking business in the *Coeur d'Alene Sun* of June 25, 1885. Allison must have moved on, because Barnard was not deterred from purchasing property in Murray on June 13, 1887.

As the emphasis in the Coeur d'Alene district shifted from gold to silver and from the North Fork to the South Fork of the Coeur d'Alene River, Barnard moved his studio to where the action was. He stayed two years in Wardner, near the Bunker Hill and Sullivan Mine, time enough to marry Norwegian-born Laura Larsen and expand his studio's business.

In 1889 he and his wife moved to Wallace. Wallace was emerging as the major commercial center of the Coeur d'Alenes and the county seat of Shoshone County. In the

---

THOMAS NATHAN BARNARD IN MONTANA (N.D.).
Barnard was working with Laton Alton Huffman in Miles City, Montana, when this photograph was taken in the early 1880s. He sent copies of it back to his family in Iowa to show them his new frontier appearance.

short term, however, the move was disastrous. Just one
year later, the Barnard Studio and its contents were
destroyed in the devastating fire of July 26, 1890, which
leveled the entire town. Barnard's reported loss of $1,000
included most of the negatives, although enough survived
from before the fire to indicate that Barnard saved part of
his collection.

Barnard's photographs during these early years reflect
the influence of Huffman and Haynes. Many of his early
landscape pictures of placer workings, townscapes, and
panoramic views taken on 5x7 and 8x10 dry-plate negatives
were undoubtedly done on speculation. Particularly arresting are the 8x10 photographs of broad, unrestricted views
of the district, including early townscapes of Wallace and
Murray taken from surrounding hills. He conveyed a
strong impression of the size of the placer workings by
including men standing beside the massive gravel faces they
were mining.

From the beginning, T. N. Barnard took photographs
to sell to the general public, and his first major publishing
effort was a 4x5 bound leather album containing forty-five
engravings made from his landscape photographs of
northern Idaho. Entitled "Coeur d'Alene Towns, Mines,
Mountains, and Lakes," it was printed in New York City
in 1891 and sold by Barnard as a souvenir in the frontier
photographic tradition.

As a portfolio of Thomas Nathan Barnard, premier
photographer of northern Idaho and the Coeur d'Alenes,
the album was complete. There were Wallace townscapes
before and after the 1890 fire, a stagecoach, a lake steamer,
the Cataldo Mission, Fort Sherman, gold and silver mines,
a snowslide, and townscapes of Burke, Wardner, Mullan,
and Murray. The album demonstrates that the cream of
Barnard's pre-1890 photographs must have survived the
1890 fire. Most, however, have not survived the
intervening years.

While T. N., as he was known to people in Wallace,
did landscape photography for sale to the general public, he
made his living from commissioned portraits that were the
mainstay of every photographic studio. He especially liked

BARNARD FAMILY, FRIENDS,
AND HOUSE, WALLACE (1898).
*A family snapshot of the Barnards
the year T. N. became mayor of
Wallace.*

group portraits because he could sell a copy to each person in the group.

Barnard had a particular strategy for dealing with the excursion steamers that came up the Coeur d'Alene River. He would arrange with the captain of the ship to announce that there was going to be a picture taken of the boat as it landed. The passengers would crowd to the shoreward side of the boat to have their picture taken, and at the landing they would order copies from the waiting photographer.

Barnard's business, like that of other small-town photographers of his time, was hardly specialized. On the one hand, he pushed his portrait work with advertisements for "life-size crayon or sepia" prints and for "ivoryette photos with platino carbon." On the other hand, he became part of a national trend to use photographs as periodical and book illustrations. In 1908, his photographs illustrated the official U.S. Government geological report on the Coeur d'Alene mining district.

While the 1890s were a time of tension and violence in the district, Barnard's personal life was that of a settled small-town family man. He and Laura had four sons: Enoch in 1890, a second son in 1892 who died in infancy, Nathan in 1896, and William in 1897. Also during this time, Barnard succumbed to mining speculation, the principal avocation of the district. He became involved in local politics and started buying real estate. In 1898, he became mayor of Wallace on the populist Citizen ticket. He was one of the local businessmen who resisted attempts by mine owners to alter the merchants' allegiance to the workers. His term of office as mayor ended on April 25, 1899, four days before the Bunker Hill and Sullivan mill was blown up—an act of violence that caused his successor to close the saloons.

With less time for photography, Barnard needed an assistant. He mentioned this to the Reverend Henry Black and his wife, Clara Stockbridge Black, both recent arrivals to the area. Clara and her sister Grace, the first woman bookkeeper in the district, had another sister, Nellie, who was a professionally trained photographer in Chicago. Black recommended her, and Barnard, mindful of the difficulty of getting trained photographic help in Idaho, wired her the offer of a job. She accepted immediately and arrived by train in Wallace on November 7, 1898.

At thirty, Nellie Stockbridge was slim, small and bespectacled, her hair knotted close to her head. Hardly the daring adventurer she was later portrayed in newspaper stories—a woman who dressed like a mucker and would risk life and limb to photograph floods, avalanches, fires, and work in the mines—she was meticulously and modestly dressed, resourceful but refined. Stories picture her riding off into the wilderness lugging fifty pounds of camera equipment. In fact, she was never seen on a horse. She never married, and her social contacts beyond her family and a few close woman friends were limited to her business. Once settled in Wallace, she seldom traveled; although her sisters eventually moved from the district, she put down roots.

While no adventurer, Nellie Stockbridge was a dedicated photographer and businesswoman. Leisure was alien to her; she worked herself to exhaustion. Stockbridge recalled in a letter to her family dated September 10, 1959, written when she was over ninety years old:

> a vivid recollection of receiving from my great Aunt Emily, a legacy of $100 when I was a very young girl. The amount was not large, but it provided me with an incentive to accumulate for future need, and it paid for the instructions through which I became a professional photographer. That has been my life work . . . .

Nellie Jane Stockbridge, born March 19, 1868, in Pana, Illinois, to railroad engineer Frederick Augustus Stockbridge and English-born Sarah Alice Fenton Stockbridge, was the second of six children. While the Stockbridge children grew up in a comfortable home, amid the fertile abundance of central Illinois, there was little extra money for frills. The children were raised to be frugal and hardworking. Their mother stretched the slim family budget to make the home

---

(Opposite) NELLIE STOCKBRIDGE AS A YOUNG WOMAN (N.D.).

attractive and inviting, and their father raised a large garden to feed the family. But when Nellie Stockbridge was still in high school, her father's eyesight began to fail, and it became apparent that the older children would need to become financially independent as soon as they were able. Necessity no doubt played a significant role over the next ten years in molding Stockbridge to her career.

From the time that she graduated from high school to the time she set out to work in the Barnard Studio, Stockbridge shared the activities and aspirations of other young women of her day—singing in the church choir, courtship, and work appropriate to her sex. She worked for a time in a millinery shop. Potential suitors were quietly, but persistently, discouraged by her mother on the pretense of the daughter's fragile health, though she almost never saw a doctor in her adult life.

Perhaps she was unfulfilled in her pursuits in Pana; perhaps she was searching for a source of financial security and independence, a concern that never left her even in old age. Sometime in her twenties, Stockbridge had the opportunity to try photo retouching at a studio in Pana, and she seized upon the idea of making photography her career. The only real evidence that she ever thought of photography in terms other than of providing her with an income is the large body of work she left behind; few other clues remain. Certainly the one fact that cannot be disputed is the seriousness with which Nellie Stockbridge undertook her chosen profession, leaving behind her a small, safe, rural community and the security of her family to move to Chicago and part with her life savings for lessons in photography.

At least one of every four professional photographers in the United States was a woman at the time Stockbridge received her training in Chicago, a high ratio in the late 1890s for any full-time profession. Women were not, even then, newcomers to the photographic industry, for they had provided inexpensive labor to manufacturers and processors of mass-produced photographic products since the technological advancement of dry plates, film negatives, and printing papers during the 1880s. Women were often preferred to men as studio assistants and retouchers because they worked for roughly half the pay. The work was also considered appropriate to the female sex because it required little heavy lifting and was conducted in relatively safe and clean surroundings. Yet formal instruction in picture taking—including lighting, exposure, chemistry, and theory, as well as retouching, trimming, and mounting—was still unusual enough in the late 1890s to suggest that Stockbridge emerged from her training in Chicago far better versed in photography than were the vast majority of practicing "professionals" of the time, regardless of sex.

When Stockbridge stepped off the train at Wallace in November, 1898, the town where she was to spend the rest of her life was still a boom town, bursting with commerce built on silver mining. It was not a tumble-down tent town like those that grew up on Prichard Creek. Wallace was lively and bustling with newness, and it had an air of affluence—if not quite respectability. The frontier still existed in the Coeur d'Alenes, but it lay with the silver ore, deep underground.

Stockbridge assisted Barnard as a retoucher when she first arrived in Wallace. She possessed the temperament to perform the painstaking, meticulous work required in touching up portraits. She soon assumed greater responsibility in the studio and probably took most of the studio portraits after 1898. Meanwhile, Barnard was serving as mayor of Wallace and spending a lot of time out of the shop. It is not clear exactly when Stockbridge took over running the studio. A newspaper article late in her life stated that she had been working for Barnard only a short time before he ran a notice announcing that "henceforth Miss Stockbridge will be in complete charge of the T. N. Barnard Studio."

After Stockbridge arrived, Barnard had more time for non-photographic activities, such as real estate promotions and mining deals. After several false starts at hotels, he built the Barnard Building on Cedar Street between Sixth and Seventh in 1907. He sold a one-quarter interest in the studio to Stockbridge on October 5, 1907, and they moved the business to the Barnard Building four months later. Barnard used the income to invest in a hog farm in the

Palouse area of eastern Washington. In April of 1908, he played his last role in Wallace city politics and was elected on the Citizen ticket to the city council.

Though only forty-seven years old in 1908, Barnard's energy was ebbing. Maybe he was already feeling the effects of the tuberculosis that would eventually kill him. He and Laura soon moved to Spokane and two years later to Los Angeles, where he died in 1916.

Stockbridge was well suited to take over the business. Her previous training in portrait photography was valuable because portraits were the mainstay of every studio's work. Yet a large part of the Barnard Studio business was advertising and promotional work commissioned by mines and local businesses. Stockbridge was called upon to photograph mines and mills, shop openings, remodelings, window displays, new buildings, fleets of shiny new trucks, and accidents (for insurance claims). In this capacity she was in a unique position to record the economic growth of the Coeur d'Alenes. Her work is particularly valuable now because she photographed the same subjects over six decades, creating a historical record that has gained importance over time.

Pictures of the Coeur d'Alene mining industries are the hallmark of the early Barnard Studio. In this work, Stockbridge followed in Barnard's footsteps. Aboveground pictures of mines and mills were often taken from high, rugged slopes in remote, inaccessible canyons. Stockbridge traveled as far as she could by buggy, then carried her equipment, or was assisted, on foot to the viewpoint. Jobs could take all day.

The real work of silver mining was done underground. There Stockbridge donned protective clothing and rode down in the man cages, water seeping and splattering on her from the shaft. Aside from being hot, dirty work, photography in the mines required a certain amount of courage and a good deal of skill as a photographer. Long exposures and special lighting had to be used, and extreme care was required to keep the camera, film, and flash dry and undamaged. Under these difficult conditions, she took pictures that rival her studio portraits in clarity.

(*Below*) PORTRAIT CAMERA, HOUSED AT THE UNIVERSITY OF IDAHO MUSEUM.
The redwood portrait camera favored by Stockbridge for studio work was made by Century Camera Company around 1903.

There was much more to running the Barnard Studio than just taking pictures. From the early 1890s, when Barnard peddled frames and specialty gift items from the "art studio," there was always a store associated with the Barnard Studio. The retail space was crammed with china, picture frames, figurines, and calendar art. Stockbridge admired beautiful, well-made things, though she rarely indulged herself with anything frivolous, and she was fiercely proud of her shop merchandise. The gift shop was an essential source of income to the studio and a hedge against economic slumps.

The Barnard Studio was located on the respectable side of Cedar Street, but the red-light district lay just a few paces away. Being in a profession that survived the booms and busts of the mining economy, the prostitutes were among Stockbridge's best customers, spending money freely on gifts from her shop for their family and friends. Stockbridge, who held firm opinions of a decidedly conservative leaning, abstained from criticism of these women. She reserved her harsh judgment for customers who asked for special favors and credit and was known to remark that the prostitutes were better behaved concerning matters of unpaid bills than many of her supposedly respectable customers.

Stockbridge worked at a frenetic pace in the shop and studio, rarely stopping to fix a meal in her small, immaculate apartment above the studio in the Barnard Building. Often she ate in restaurants. At the studio, in her quick, soft-spoken, and practical manner, she waited on customers, placed orders with salesmen, received merchandise, made inventories, and kept her own books in addition to taking pictures at the back of her shop. She did not have much time for small talk.

When the Barnard Studio was moved to the Barnard Building in 1908, the early portrait negatives were destroyed and the studio's working file of particularly interesting negatives was culled. From this file Stockbridge made contact prints and mounted pictures and postcards that were sold at the studio's gift shop, as Barnard had done before her. She continued to add to and discard from this working file for the next fifty-five years. During that time, the working file began to take on her imprint as a photographer and preservationist. To a core collection of early Coeur d'Alene pictures taken by Barnard were added pictures taken by Stockbridge of businesses, architecture, church groups, schools, parades, picnics, mining activity, and cataclysmic events that changed people's lives such as fires, floods, and avalanches. At the end of her life the working file included several thousand negatives, all considered by Stockbridge to be of historical and aesthetic interest. By advertising the Barnard Studio's historical photographs, she promoted an awareness of the district's past.

Stockbridge carefully filed working negatives in fresh envelopes and developed a labeling system for them. Constant or careless handling deteriorates negatives of any kind and introduces the risk of breaking glass negatives, but her meticulous darkroom techniques and special care in storing the working negatives actually helped preserve them.

Although Stockbridge had a number of different assistants in her career, she was reluctant to allow them to take pictures, and she maintained strict control over the printing and developing processes. As a result, there is a remarkable consistency of quality throughout the collection. The studio's negatives were always properly developed and processed so that there was no excessive chemical residue on the negatives to contribute to deterioration over the years.

Stockbridge learned which cameras and materials worked best for her, and she did not experiment widely. She favored her 1903 Century portrait camera and field cameras that used dry-plate glass negatives (she actually used dry-plate negatives occasionally for portraits until World War II) and did not use flexible film negatives at the studio until 1918, although they were available earlier.

When Nellie Stockbridge was in her eighties, she lost sight in one eye because of a detached retina. Unwilling to have her assistants take pictures for her, she continued to take them with a combination of experience and guesswork and to instruct her helpers in proper developing and printing techniques. She wrote her family:

EARLY PICTURE OF THE BARNARD STUDIO GIFT SHOP (N.D.).
The woman tending the store is tentatively identified as Nellie's sister Grace.

[Photography] has been my life work . . . . They have been long, often wearing and always confining hours. For sixty years I have had sole responsibility of a studio and gift store. Always I have stood alone. Looking back over the long trail I have traveled, there comes a remembrance of the time when it was a struggle to get and to keep something to depend upon when the infirmities of age would prevent further activity. [Ibid., 6]

She was active in the studio and in good health until months before her death at the age of ninety-seven. Nellie Stockbridge died May 22, 1965, leaving behind a complete and intact photographic legacy of a mining district—her life's work and the work of her partner, T. N. Barnard.

Thomas Barnard was a romantic in his move west, in choosing photography as his profession, in his mining speculation, and in his populist politics. Through his early pictures we see the district as he did—full of promise and enterprise. Stockbridge built upon this foundation, drawing from her professional training and applying it to frontier conditions. She recorded the world as she found it, consistently, faithfully, for six decades. Her instinct for the importance of preserving the present for the future was a rare quality on the frontier, rare as the fragile glass negatives she kept for future generations.

NELLIE STOCKBRIDGE IN HER NINETIES (N.D.).

GOLD MINING

✦

T HE STAMPEDE to the Coeur d'Alenes that took place in the
winter and spring of 1883–84 was largely created by a
brochure entitled "In the Gold Fields of the Coeur
d'Alenes." It was published by the Northern Pacific Railroad to
stimulate traffic on the new line that looped north of the Coeur
d'Alenes en route to Tacoma. The gold strike that prompted the
publication was made on Prichard Creek, a tributary of the North
Fork of the Coeur d'Alene River, by A. J. Prichard in the fall of 1883.

The promotional pamphlet urged any man who could lift a
pickax to take a ride west on the "only line running to the
celebrated gold fields." For $77.18, a person could travel first class
from St. Paul, Minnesota, to Belknap, Montana. But from there
the stampeder was on his own to face more than twenty-five miles
of roadless, densely forested mountain trail, with twenty feet of ice
and snow at the pass in the long winter season.

The peak of the gold rush took place in January and February
of 1884. Stampeders outfitted themselves with snowshoes, toboggans, and enough bacon, flour, beans, and whiskey to meet any
scarcity or misfortune they might encounter during the winter.
Their destination was Eagle City, the first boom town to grow up

near the site of Prichard's discovery. To reach the North Fork from Belknap with a full load of supplies took four to five days, and as many as three hundred toboggans crossed the mountains each day at the peak of the rush.

Contemporary magazine journalist Eugene Smalley reported that five thousand stampeders—miners, merchants, prostitutes, and packers—came by rail and trail from east and west in 1883 and 1884 in hopes of profiting from the gold diggings. All along gold-rich Prichard Creek and its tributaries stampeders set up in shacks and gaudy tents. There they ate beans and bacon, drank whiskey, and awaited the thaw.

Murrayville, later called Murray, consisted of a heavy concentration of tents and hovels near the richest placer claims on Prichard Creek. It was founded on January 22, 1884, during the first winter of the rush. By late summer of that year, the most promising quartz mines were producing, and the town's population had grown to 2,500. Smalley, writing in the October, 1884, issue of *Century Magazine,* described Murray in the summer of 1884:

> It is composed of a hideous half-mile-long street of huts, shanties and tents, with three or four cross-streets that run against the steep slopes after a few rods progress . . . . A more unattractive place than Murray I have seldom seen. Stumps and half-charred logs encumber the streets, and serve as seats for the inhabitants. Chairs can only be found in the principal gambling establishments. Every second building is a drinking saloon . . . . The town was full of men out of employment and out of money, who hung about the saloons and cursed the camp in

(Overleaf) THE MOTHER LODE BOYS (188?). (PRINT COPIED ONTO GLASS NEGATIVE AT THE STUDIO.)
This photograph is often titled the "Spirit of the Coeur d'Alenes." Three Washington Territory farmers staked this quartz claim early in the rush. "The happiest trio to be found in all the camps of the Coeur d'Alenes," wrote Eugene Smalley in Century Magazine *in 1884, because it was generally believed that the Mother Lode was located at the heart of all the gold in the region.*

(Opposite) MURRAY (1890).
Barnard established his first studio in Murray at the peak of gold fever. By the time this picture was taken in 1890, placer deposits had been worked over or abandoned and miners had moved on to the silver- and lead-producing properties on the South Side. Barnard followed suit, moving his studio to Wardner and then to Wallace.

(Below) SNYBAR CABIN (1897).
Barnard moved his studio from the gold fields to the silver towns of the Coeur d'Alenes early on, but photographs such as this one of a prospector of the SnyBar claim suggest his continued interest in all aspects of mining in the district.

all styles of profanity known to the miners' vocabulary.

Though the stampeders came from every conceivable class, and many were recent French and Italian immigrants, the miners of Murray reached an early consensus about Chinese labor in the district. The Chinese willingness to work for low wages fostered deep resentment among wage-earning miners. The miners were not the only members of the working class who hated the Chinese. It was said that Molly b'Damn, then reigning madam of Murray's red-light district, made eloquent pleas from horseback throughout the district in favor of banning Chinese. Adam Aulbach, an itinerant newspaperman who established himself in the district early in the rush, expressed local sentiment in an editorial appearing March 22, 1884, in the *Coeur d'Alene Sun*.

> The fiat has gone forth that no celestial can ever gaze upon the wooded gulches of the Coeur d'Alenes and live. This camp, like Leadville, will never feel the curse of cheap coolie labor . . . . If he insists on coming, however, let him bring a roast hog, plenty of fire crackers and colored paper and all the essentials of a first class Chinese funeral. He needn't bother to bring the corpse. It will be in readiness.

Despite the big talk, the citizens of Murray prided themselves that Murray had less crime and violence than large towns, and Murray was a peaceful camp by western standards, though nearly everyone was armed. The occasional homicides were attributed to transient low-life characters; mining disputes were usually settled in court (there was an ample supply of lawyers) rather than with firearms.

———————

ARCHIE SMITH IN FRONT OF HIS CABIN (N.D.).
Smith and his partner Rufus Dunlap worked thousands of dollars' worth of gold from their placer claim on the upper East Fork of Eagle Creek over a period of forty years, using pans, rockers, and sluices. A stereograph was probably made from this double print, which, when viewed through a stereoscopic viewer, gave this scene a three-dimensional quality.

Two important events established Murray as the center of the Coeur d'Alenes in the early 1880s. The first was the completion of roads between Murray and the railroad lines at Thompson Falls, Montana, and between Murray and the steamship landing on the Coeur d'Alene River. The second important event was the transfer of the Shoshone county seat from Pierce, scene of a rush in 1860, to Murray. Because of the gold strike, Murray had grown to be the largest town in Shoshone County by 1884, giving its citizens some political clout. In that year the Idaho territorial legislature decided to move the county seat from Pierce, a boom-to-bust town on the verge of extinction located three hundred miles south of Murray. A special election was called in June of 1885, and two-thirds of the 1,537 votes cast favored a county seat at Murray. For thirteen years, until Wallace became the county seat, Murray was the official political and legal center of the Coeur d'Alenes.

The spring thaw in 1884 revealed that the placer deposits in the main channel of Prichard Creek were buried under twenty-five feet of overlaying gravel, which discouraged simple sluice and rocker mining methods. Most of the mining in 1884 and 1885 was therefore carried out on ledges along the rim of upper Prichard Creek and in the gulches of its tributaries. An ancient creek bed called Old Wash Channel ran parallel to and above Prichard Creek, intersecting all the tributary gulches on the north side of the main creek. It was from Old Wash gravels, dispersed erratically through these gulches, that most of the nuggets and coarse gold were taken by simple placer methods.

Water is essential to all methods of placer mining. Water washed over gravel separates heavy gold from lighter silt and rock. Gold settles to the bottom of the watery gravel mixture and the rest is washed away. This simple principle is the basis of all placer gold-mining techniques, including panning, rocking, sluicing, and hydraulicking.

Without proper amounts of water, claims could not be worked. But mining along the North Fork could not begin until the spring runoffs had subsided, and by May the smaller gulches were dry.

A number of highly speculative schemes were proposed to transport water so that the Old Wash sites could be mined on a large scale, but none of the instigators of these plans met with the success they hoped for. In 1885, the Bed Rock Flume Company started work on an enormous sixteen-foot-wide sluice built on bedrock down the channel of Prichard Creek with railroad ties for riffles and using heavy machinery to lift boulders out of the way. Although it was an ingenious plan to use the main flow of the creek to carry gravel through the sluice, financing fell through before the project was completed.

Dr. Morganer, an overbearing entrepreneur from St. Louis, attempted to build flumes six feet wide and four feet deep aboveground to carry water to the Old Wash Channel and Prichard Creek diggings. He won the contempt and distrust of the local population by paying his workers in scrip, to be redeemed in cash when the ditch started to make profits. January 2, 1886, a poem appeared in the *Murray Sun:*

> The year past was fraught with changed events of every day,/ The early topic of the spring, When will Morganer pay?/ All held his scrip with ardent grip, praising him who giveth,/ But doubting still, with right good will, if its redeemer liveth.

The project was never finished, as financing again ran out. Some residents of the area later conceded that Morganer's plan might have worked if he had not so antagonized the local citizens.

Over half a million dollars in gold was taken from the district in 1884 and 1885 by small-scale labor-intensive methods employing pans, rockers, and sluices, but by 1886 the yields were beginning to falter under the limitations of these methods and inexperienced management.

After the first wave of disappointed prospectors set out on other adventures, several cash-poor miners found

THE MOTHER LODE MILL AT LITTLEFIELD (1890).
Quartz milling nearly died out in the 1890s but was revived sporadically whenever the price of gold went up a few dollars an ounce. Nine stamp mills and one Spanish arrastra were working near Murray at the time this picture was taken. The Mother Lode used a Fraser and Chambers #44 ten-stamp mill.

themselves with quartz claims rich in minerals that could not be mined by placer methods. Quartz-imbedded gold had to be extracted from the ore through crushing and refining, and that took capital. Owners of these claims were faced with selling out to whoever made the best offer or finding outside financing to buy essential water rights, refining equipment, and transportation for mining and milling their ore. Such a claim was the Mother Lode.

Newspaper editor Adam Aulbach, eyewitness to the development on the North Side, reported in his newspaper in 1891 that the Mother Lode Company had been estab-

lished in 1885 by the claim's owners for just such development. The group of Washington Territory farmers turned prospectors established the Mother Lode claim early in the gold stampede and for many months they

sat and watched the gold slab, going hungry at times, but always courteous to visitors. One handsome offer after another for this mining property was refused. They were afraid to sell for fear there might be more wealth in the mine than the offer amounted to.

When the owners decided at last to develop their own

claim, they installed an arrastra—a huge horizontal stone wheel—to pulverize the gold-impregnated quartz ore that had been mined with pick and shovel from the steep hillside. Next the company bought a stamp mill consisting of five vertical rods lifted by cams on a shaft turned by a large waterwheel. Although the stamp mill was a rather inefficient method of milling, ore high in gold content made the process worthwhile when the stamp mill and arrastra were used together, the mill crushing the ore and the arrastra grinding it to a fine powder.

The Mother Lode company was paying its investors dividends by the late 1880s, and in 1891 Aulbach further reported:

> the mine had yielded $200,000 up to the present day, and is scarcely opened up. Nuggets weighing as much as twenty and twenty-seven ounces of pure gold were hammered out of the quartz.

However, the district's total production of gold had dropped to the lowest level since the rush. It was rumored that the gold fields were played out. The mood in Murray was grim and many houses stood empty. Quartz milling, Murray's only hope for economic revival, was hampered by unprofitable methods, high grading (the stealing of mineral-bearing ore by workers), and absentee ownership. "I would rather die on Broadway than live in Murray," a statement attributed to Vivian Green, owner of the Golden Chest Mine, probably overstates the disadvantages of living in the district, yet most mine owners did not live in the Coeur

(Opposite) ARIZONA PLACER MINE, HYDRAULICKING IN DREAM GULCH (N.D.).
The men with the poles at right stood poised to dislodge boulders from the cemented gravel face. The man on the left was hydraulicking with a small hand-held monitor.

(Right) ARIZONA PLACER MINE SHOWING SLUICES AND RIFFLES (N.D.).
By April 1884, eleven claims in the district had hit bedrock using variations of the sluicing method, and every miner in the district was busy building sluices, digging drainage ditches, and preparing claims for mining by this relatively inexpensive method.

d'Alenes. Their absenteeism and neglect restricted effective quartz mining over the years.

After 1890, several sporadic attempts were made to mine Prichard Creek with hydraulics—blasting away hillsides with water and washing the gravels into sluices—but the lack of water remained a problem. The consolidation of nearly all the gold-mining properties in the district in the early 1900s under the management of Barry Hillard at the Coeur d'Alene Mining Company finally made possible a unified, comprehensive plan for mining the remaining placer gold. In 1917, the Coeur d'Alene Mining Company leased the consolidated properties to the Yukon Gold Company for dredging.

In the fall of 1917, the Yukon Gold Company, backed by Guggenheim money, moved a large dredge from Alaska to Prichard Creek near the mouth of Dream Gulch. When assembled, the dredge was 106 feet long and 44 feet wide, and it floated in nine feet of water. Six electric motors powered the dredge twenty-four hours a day, nearly every day for eight and one-half years. Its seventy-six large steel dredge buckets overturned creek bed from Dream Gulch to Accident Gulch and back again. At Murray, it dredged up Gold Street and piled the tailings on Main Street.

The Yukon Gold Company located its offices at the old Murray courthouse, and the company's payroll breathed some life back into the town for a time. The company took $1,270,000 in gold from Prichard Creek gravel beds for a profit of $500,000. The combined gold production from all gold-mining methods over forty years was worth more than $4,000,000, but the highest production for any single year was in 1885, at the hands of early prospectors, before hydraulics and dredging were introduced to the Coeur d'Alenes.

The stampeders who fought their way over the pass in the middle of winter in 1883–84 in their determination to get to the gold first were best rewarded. But prospecting fever did not stop there; even before the gold rush had peaked, stampeders discovered that "all that glitters is not gold." It was the glint of silver-bearing galena ore that would put the Coeur d'Alenes permanently on the map of America's richest mining areas.

PLACER MINING, DELTA (N.D.).
Shallow creek placers, such as this one, were hydraulicked with water reservoirs only thirty-five to one hundred feet above the monitors. Large monitors were bolted down to heavy timbers or braced against bedrock.

PLACER MINES, Delta, Alaska

SILVER MINING

⚜

T HE CHANGE from gold to silver mining in the Coeur
d'Alene district in the late 1880s meant not only a transformation of the independent, self-employed prospector
into a wage-earning company man, but also a complete change in
mining techniques and equipment. While the gold prospector used
pans, rockers, sluices, and hoses to get at his metal, the silver miner
used dynamite, drills, mine cars, and hoists. The trek from the gold-
rush placer mines of the North Fork of the Coeur d'Alene River to
the hard-rock silver and lead mines of the South Fork was an
irrevocable step from the American frontier to the benefits and
restrictions of the industrial revolution. Those who did not — or
could not — make that step had few places left to "rush."

Hard-rock mining of silver and lead began in the Coeur d'Alenes
in 1885, just as machine drilling of blasting holes was introduced.
Hand drilling continued in some of the smaller mines and in
exploration work until the early 1900s. Hand drilling was called
"jacking" after the "Cousin Jacks," a term applied to Cornish miners
because they seemed always to have a "cousin" ready to come from
Cornwall to work in the mines. They and the Irish made up a
plurality of hard-rock miners in the West until the end of the

century. The "Cousin Jacks" were viewed as professionals, following a family and ethnic tradition that had begun in the tin mines of Cornwall.

A miner could work alone at "single-jacking," twisting a ¾-inch drill with one hand and swinging a three-pound hammer with the other. Single-jacking was exhausting work, difficult for even the most experienced men to maintain for hours on end. "Double-jacking" by two men was more common, both because it was more efficient and because it was easier on the miners. One man would swing an eight-pound hammer with both hands on the thirty-three-inch handle, while his partner would twist, clean, and change the one-inch drill. A truncated swing from shoulder height was the most effective and was the only way to maintain the pace of fifty hits per minute that was the goal. At that rate and in the flickering light of a few tallow candles, the slightest error could mean smashed fingers or a broken arm. Most hard-rock miners carried scars of such mishaps.

Drilling and blasting were always the most respected jobs underground because they demanded the most skill. Learned only through experience and under the strain of constant danger, these skills determined whether the miner, and ultimately the mine, was a success. Strong drillers had quite a reputation, which they could test at highly popular drilling competitions at the Fourth of July celebrations in mining districts. On July 4, 1913, in Wardner, the largest crowd ever to attend such contests in the Coeur d'Alenes watched a spirited competition won by Siligo and St. Germaine, who drilled 46-13/16 inches in Vermont granite in the regulation fifteen minutes. These highly trained teams spent months before the event preparing the right "steel" (or drills) and practicing the exacting competition routine, which included changing roles every thirty seconds without missing a beat in the rhythm (which some teams pushed to seventy-seven strokes per minute).

(Overleaf) Tin Cup group, Hercules Mine (1905).
A posed photograph shows double-jack hand drilling in the Hercules Mine. No regular miner would ever wear a white shirt and tie underground.

The use of explosives transformed mining from an arduous occupation to a hazardous one. No matter how skilled a miner might be, a less experienced co-worker might blow them both to pieces. The familiarity that miners developed with dynamite never bred contempt for its power, and it made them a tough group outside the mine. The extracurricular use of a little "Giant Powder," as dynamite was first

Single-jacking contest at Mullan (1940).
Machine drills had been in use for years when this old-timer took on the field in a single-jacking contest at the Mullan '49ers Days celebration.

called when introduced in America, punctuated the workers' requests for better laboring conditions.

In developing dynamite in 1866, Swedish inventor Alfred Nobel found a way to combine the highly explosive and equally unstable nitroglycerine with an absorbent compound. The resultant explosive could be jolted, jarred, and even burned without exploding. So inert was dynamite that it needed a powerful blasting cap to detonate it. Dynamite was a blessing to miners because it was more stable and safer to handle than its predecessors, such as black powder and nitrogylcerin.

The use of dynamite, however, was not without problems. If left standing in warm storage it would start leaking liquid nitroglycerin, which explodes at the slightest bump. On the other hand, it sometimes did not explode when it was supposed to and would become an unsuspected danger to those who came later. A less obvious danger was the creation of carbonic oxide and nitrous gases by the dynamite explosions. These gases would not affect a candle's burning, the traditional method by which miners determined whether a mine was safe to work, but could knock a man unconscious.

Much of the underground work has remained unchanged since the introduction of water-fed hammer drills in 1918. A shaft was sunk, off which tunnels led to various locations on the ore vein. The mining of a vein was done in the stopes, cut above the tunnel, so that gravity would bring the loose ore down a frame chute to the tunnel, where it would fall into cars for transportation to the central shaft and out of the mine. At the end of the stope, the miners drilled blasting holes into the "face" or wall of rock that contained the ore vein. The holes were drilled three to five feet deep and one to three feet apart, in a pattern designed to blast out as much rock as possible in the best size for hauling out of the mine.

At the turn of the century, George Leyner developed a pneumatic drill powered by compressed air pumped in through one of the two connecting hoses. The other hose carried water that was forced through the hollow drill "steel" and cleaned out the hole as it was drilled. Not only was Leyner's drill a major technological advance, but the compressed air helped to ventilate the drift and the water greatly reduced the dust. Such water drills were introduced in the Coeur d'Alenes in 1918, replacing the "Wiggle-Tail" buzzy, a dry pneumatic drill that was hand-rotated and nicknamed the "widow maker" for its lethal tendency to loosen rock from the ceiling during drilling.

Machine drills weighed between 95 and 150 pounds and had to be mounted on horizontal or vertical columns when in use. The columns themselves weighed several hundred pounds and were secured in place by jack-screwing them against the walls, ceiling, and floor. These unwieldy columns were replaced in the early 1940s by the "jackleg," a hydraulic attachment on the rear of a more advanced and lighter drill that supported it against the floor and provided continuous pressure as the drill penetrated the face.

Once drilled, the one- to two-inch-wide holes were filled with eight-inch- to twelve-inch-long sticks of dynamite, made of 40 to 95 percent nitroglycerine soaked in a sawdust-like absorbent. These sticks were slit down the side so they would break open and fill the hole completely with powder when tamped into the hole with a wooden or copper ram-

(Right) Butte and Coeur d'Alene Mine, men drilling (1928). *Stockbridge exposed the film for several seconds before she flashed the lamp to catch these miners and their compressed-air drill, probably an Ingersoll Water Leyner. Some miners used their pipes to ignite the blasting charges.*

(Below) Morning Mine interior showing cages (n.d.). *These man cages at the end of a single wire cable were the only way in and out of the mines. Safety clogs stopped a falling cage if the wire broke, but a greater danger was being slammed against the machinery at the top of the shaft by an inattentive operator or runaway hoist.*

rod. Then they were topped with mercury fulminate blasting caps, their fuses hanging down the face. Clay was tamped on top to hold the charge in place. The fuses were cut in different lengths so the holes fired in the correct order, with the ones in the center going first. Miners commonly wore fuses as belts, and if a miner fell asleep during the lunch break, he ran the risk of having his fuse belt lit and ending up with a hot seat.

After the miners were warned with the traditional "Fire in the hole!" the miner lit the fuse and retreated to the central shaft. It became the practice to fire the round at the end of the work shift and then leave the mine to allow the smoke to clear. One round at the end of a drift brought down six tons of rock and moved the drift forward about three feet. It was very important to count the number of blasts to make sure that all the holes had blown. Otherwise, the next shift of miners might find themselves drilling into an unexploded stick of dynamite, an experience they were not likely to remember.

In many mines, the floor next to the face was covered with sheet metal before blasting. The smooth surface made it much easier for the shovelers to clean up the rock after the blast and materially increased output.

When they came to the stope after the blast, the shovelers, known as "muckers," had first to "wet down" the area to settle the dust and then "bar down" by using a pinch bar to pull down any loose rock from the ceiling. Once they could work without being hit by falling rock, the muckers carried the ore by wheelbarrow or scoop to a wooden chute called a "transfer raise" that carried it down to the main tunnel below. The ore could be held in the chutes and then released into cars on the track below. One of the most dangerous jobs in the mine was unclogging the chute when it jammed. If the hang-up could not be loosened by beating on the chute or "barring" through the sides of the chute, one brave (or foolish) soul had to crawl up the chute, plant some dynamite, and get out before it blew or the rock spontaneously freed itself.

Once full, the one-ton cars were pushed or hauled by mule and later by electric locomotives to the central shaft,

where they were rolled directly into the cages or emptied into pockets next to the shaft. Then a heavily reinforced cage, called a "skip," was positioned in the shaft below the pocket and the ore released through a steel gate into it. When the skip was full, it was raised to the surface and the ore was transferred by conveyor belt or ore car to the mill.

Muckers were usually not as skilled as the miners doing the drilling and blasting; indeed, they were often apprentices learning the trade. After he could differentiate between plain rock and ore, the mucker had to learn "to fill the heel of the shovel, the toe will take care of itself." One of the major causes of the mining wars of the 1890s was the desire of the mine owners to pay the muckers less than the other miners. The unions, maintaining that the difficulty and danger were the same for both types of work, wanted them paid the same.

Experience and skill were required by the men who timbered the stopes every six feet or so as the rock was taken out. Heavy, foot-square timbers were dragged into the drifts and skillfully placed to form arches. As the vein was mined upward, the timbered drifts below became wooden catacombs that were later filled up with waste rock as the work progressed, a mining method extensively used in the Coeur d'Alenes called "horizontal stoping with stull sets and fill."

Large amounts of timber were used in the Coeur d'Alene mines for this work, for supports in tunnels and stopes, for enclosing shafts and chutes, and for railroad ties. In the early years, the ready supply of timber in the nearby forests made the adoption of this particular approach to mining possible. Timber was preferable to concrete because it could yield under pressure without breaking, and preferable to iron because it did not rust. However, it could rot and did catch fire, which was the greatest danger in the mines because a fire would consume oxygen and form carbon monoxide, killing the miners.

SUCCESS MINE INTERIOR, WALLACE (N.D.).
Ore came thundering down out of the chute on the left and into the ore car on the tracks. Climbing up to unclog the chute was one of the terrors of early miners.

366-C

The demand for timber was such that it was not long before the slopes nearest the mines were stripped bare and the companies had to go farther for the fir, pine, spruce, and larch used underground. When cars returned to the drifts after taking the ore out, they often carried the pre-cut timber used in stoping.

The big ore skips and smaller man cages called "chippies" were raised and lowered on single wire ropes or cables by electric or steam hoists. Their motors turned huge drums, around which were wrapped the ⅜-inch or ⅝-inch thick flat wire cable that was attached to the top of the cage. This cable became elastic when stretched out over hundreds of feet, and the loaded cage on the end moved up and down as if on the end of a rubber band. The cages carried everyone that went into and came out of the mine. Their design has been basically the same since the beginning of mining in the Coeur d'Alenes.

The basic method of communication between the miners below and the hoistman above was a simple bell code. A bell hung in the "hoist shanty," and a long rope attached to the clapper extended down the shaft next to the cage. One yank on the rope meant to hoist away or stop, if the cage was in motion; five bells meant "blasting" or "ready to shoot," which told the hoistman to hold the cage at that level ready for the miners to get in after they lit their fuses. The bell code was displayed on each level of the mine to prevent mistakes in communication.

The experience of going down in a cage (at a rate more rapid than an elevator—up to 1,200 feet per minute) has not changed. It is a kaleidoscope of dulled sounds, musty dampness, and the occasional flash of light as a mining level flies by. The ever present water drips down the shaft and splashes on the cage and the miners within. But for all the water, the darkness, and the occasional falling rock on the cage roof, nothing is as frightening as the thought of a falling, runaway cage. From early days, each cage had an automatic brake of sharp teeth, called "dogs," that bit into the wooden guides which were bolted to the shaft timbers if the cage fell out of control. Fatal accidents occurred when the safety catches on the fast-moving cages did not work or

when a hoistman's error slammed the cage up into the "sheave wheel." Anyone in the open cages not careful to keep himself clear of the shaft walls rushing by would quickly lose limb or life. The danger exists: ten minutes after midnight on October 6, 1936, the worst accident ever to occur at the Morning Mine near Mullan happened when the wire rope in the main shaft broke, killing ten miners. The flat ⅜x4½-inch rope broke with a load of six tons, although its "breaking strength" was seventy-two tons. A coroner's jury found that it was an "unavoidable accident."

Large-scale sources of inexpensive power were indispensable to the workings of the complex machinery required in the mines. The thirty-three-foot Pelton water wheel that powered the Grouse Gulch compressor for the Morning Mine was the largest in the world when it began operation on December 8, 1900. A mile-and-a-half-long wooden flume and two pipes of similar length brought water to run the wheel from the Coeur d'Alene River and two nearby creeks. The big Pelton wheel and its two twelve-foot companions developed 1,100 horsepower to run two fifty-drill Rix compressors. Air in them was compressed to ninety pounds per square inch and held at that pressure in a 12,000-cubic-foot underground storage area.

At the time it was installed, the twenty-three-ton machinery provided the compressed air to power pneumatic drills, run the hoists, and provide cooling and ventilation. Even after the introduction of electricity, compressed air continued to be used to power drills underground. It helped ventilate the mine, did not produce sparks that could set fires, and powered drills that were superior to electric ones.

While some mines had developed local sources for electricity in the Wallace area as early as 1890, not until 1903 was the mining district provided with a regular source of electrical power, when transmission lines were erected from the hydroelectric plant at Spokane Falls. Electricity was cheaper than other sources of power, such as steam, and made possible more light in the workplace. By eliminating the need for steam engines underground, electric power helped cool the mine. Electric locomotives pulled the mine cars and electric hoists lifted the cages.

The introduction of electricity brought many benefits, but it could not improve the quality of air underground. Deep in the lead and silver mines, the air was difficult to breathe and dangerous to the miners. Stale air full of carbon dioxide could suffocate a person in minutes, as could carbon monoxide from the lamps and explosions. Fumes from unburnt nitroglycerine, the fine quartz dust left after blasting, and the lead compounds in the ore were debilitating and disabling. Breathing the quartz dust caused silicosis, known as "miner's con," a growth of fibrous nodules in the lungs that impairs breathing. Victims felt a shortness of breath and started coughing. As their lung problem worsened, they weakened and became unable to work. The lucky ones were given surface jobs. The unlucky ones found themselves laid off from the only work they knew. Death from miner's con was not uncommon, contributing to the high mortality rate from mining, which averaged 2.47 deaths per thousand miners in Idaho between 1903 and 1908. The introduction of technological innovation to mining had its human price.

When it was determined that ore in a mine was workable, the owner's next step was to acquire or build a mill to concentrate the ore and thereby reduce the freight charges on the ore sent to the smelter. A mill was built down the slope from the entrance, or portal, of the mine to take advantage of the force of gravity in carrying the heavy ore through the milling process. The concentrator, as the mill was called, was used to separate the minerals from the rock in which they were embedded. There was a constant effort to increase the per-ton value of the concentrate sent to the smelter by recovering as much of the mineral content as possible from the ore.

The first concentrators, built before 1890, depended extensively on sorting ore by hand, and the mills recovered about 70 percent of the silver and lead values. While these early "rockhouses" with their crude machinery lost large quantities of minerals, they were not very expensive. By the turn of the century, the milling process had been refined to recover 90 percent of the minerals in the ore.

Concentrating began with crushing the ore as it came from the mine and filtering it through selective grids called "grizzlies" into ball mills with eight-foot-diameter rotating drums containing iron or steel shot the size of cannon balls. The ore was ground to a fine sand that ended up in large flotation tanks for the chemical and physical removal of silver and lead. The flotation process became more selective in 1922, making it possible to recover zinc from large bodies of the ore. Previously regarded as troublesome and called "black jack" or "poison" by miners, zinc became overnight an equal to silver and lead as a product of the Coeur d'Alene district.

The mineral concentrate removed from a specified level of the flotation tank by means of chemical precipitate was then stored for shipment to the smelter. Until 1917, when the first Bunker Hill smelter was built in Kellogg, this meant railroad shipment to Montana, Colorado, the Pacific Coast, or even farther away. The sand that was left, called tailings or waste, was then either carried back into the mines to fill up mined-out stopes or moved to huge waste dumps.

The Hercules Mill, built in December of 1905, was the most efficient in the Coeur d'Alenes for its time. Mine owner Harry Day and his head millwright, Frank Franz, had toured other mills in the West to study their recovery methods. Day bought the worthless fourteen-acre Trade Dollar claim downhill from the Hercules portal in Gorge Gulch and built there a 150-foot-high mill of Douglas fir on a stone foundation. The wooden construction of mining mills made them highly flammable, and the Hercules operated for only four years before burning down in the summer of 1909.

During the period from the discovery of the Coeur d'Alene silver and lead mines in the mid-1880s to the end of the century, their ownership generally changed from prospector–discoverer to financier–entrepreneur to the corporation. The most important exception was the Hercules, which was controlled by the family of the discoverer throughout its rich history.

The most successful mine of the Coeur d'Alenes, owned by the Bunker Hill and Sullivan Mining Company, is a classic example of a changing pattern of ownership. The Bunker Hill was discovered in 1885 by disappointed gold prospectors who wandered out of the North Fork drainage around Murray to the slopes of the South Fork of the Coeur d'Alene River. The lucky prospector was Noah Kellogg, who, having brought back some galena ore from Milo Gulch to show friends around Murray, did not seem quite certain what it was. Others did know and joined up with him, although his choice of companions to share his good fortune later caused trouble because he neglected to include the men who had originally grubstaked him and who were entitled to half of any claim he made. They eventually won a court case against Kellogg and received a one-quarter share of the value of the prospects that Kellogg had found.

While Kellogg was lucky (local legend claimed that his donkey found the ore), Jim Wardner was clever. Hearing of Kellogg's strike, he went immediately to Milo Gulch and claimed the water rights of the drainage. Control of water rights was then, and has been since, of major importance in mining affairs. It gave Wardner a powerful bargaining position when he sat down with Kellogg's group to talk about the future of the strike. Wardner quickly became the entrepreneur of the group, arranging financing from Governor Samuel T. Hauser of Montana and shipping ore samples out for testing.

The pace of events quickened. A contract was signed with a smelter in Montana, and a narrow-gauge railroad was built up the South Fork toward the mine. The ore tested high in both silver and lead. But even with Hauser's help, the group did not have the financial resources necessary to develop the mine. They sold the mine in 1887 to a

---

HERCULES MINE AND MILL, BURKE (1907).
The Hercules Mill burned down four years after it was built in 1905. Sparks from the heavy metal machinery or from the primitive electrical systems started the fires that were common among the wooden mills of the Coeur d'Alenes.

GROUSE GULCH COMPRESSOR, MORNING MINE (N.D.).
The size of the man in the center of the picture indicates the size of this enormous Pelton water wheel, which powered the compressors for the entire Morning Mine. This Pelton wheel was the epitome of the first wave of Industrial Revolution technology, when additional power was obtained by making everything larger.

Portland, Oregon, financier, Simeon Reed, for $650,000, of which Noah Kellogg received $150,000. Reed knew he needed an experienced professional mining engineer to develop his property and asked John Hays Hammond, then well known for his work in California, to take the job. Hammond declined, but he recommended—and Reed hired—Victor M. Clement, a California mining engineer.

Within a short time, national financiers and professional mine managers replaced the independent and untrained men who had made the original discovery. A mine the size of the Bunker Hill required large amounts of capital and sophisticated professional expertise, which was just not available in the Coeur d'Alenes at that time. Financiers like Simeon Reed and professional engineers like Clement, Hammond, and later Fred Bradley were the ones to profit from Noah Kellogg's discovery. All of the engineers also invested in the mine and thereby profited doubly from their relationship to it. Kellogg himself remained a well-known character in the area but soon used up the money he had made from the discovery.

The Bunker Hill quickly became the largest mine in the district. Fred Bradley was president during the first two decades of the twentieth century and built the Bunker Hill's own smelter in 1917 to free the mine from its dependence on the Guggenheims' near monopoly of American lead smelting.

Not all of the early mining entrepreneurs were as successful as the owners of the Bunker Hill. In the case of the Morning Mine, the mine was a success but the rest of the owner's financial empire collapsed. The mine, two miles southwest of Mullan, was located in July of 1884 by George Goode and was one of the first silver and lead mines in the Coeur d'Alene district. In 1887, Goode sold it for $12,600 to Charles and Warren Hussey, brothers with banks in Murray, Wallace, and Spokane. During the next two years, they built a two-and-a-half-mile-long bucket tramway from the mine entrance to their mill at Mullan, where they concentrated 170 tons of ore a day.

Warren Hussey was one of the major bankers of the area and the first president of the Spokane Mining Ex-

change, after he made a good deal of money as the major banker of the gold rush into the North Fork. Yet on December 17, 1890, his financial empire collapsed, closing the Bank of Wallace, the Spokane National Bank, and the Morning Mine. Fortunately for the depositors in Hussey's banks, the Morning Mine was a successful property and was sold from receivership for $400,000. The money was used to pay off the depositors.

The Morning Mine was also the site of an attempt

unique in the Coeur d'Alenes to run a mine as a cooperative. In 1894, D. B. Huntley, the lessor, signed up 150 men who would share in the profits from their work. When their daily share reached only $2.68, somewhat lower than the prevailing wage in the area, the miners' union protested and the experiment closed down.

In the early 1900s, the Morning Mine was bringing in an annual yield of over a million dollars, but the owners at that time did not have the capital to follow the veins below the five levels that by then had been worked out. Their need for capital coincided with the extraordinary effort by Charles Sweeny, backed by Rockefeller money, to buy up the whole Coeur d'Alene mining district. From 1903 to 1905, the newly organized Federal Mining and Smelting Company, with Sweeny as its first president, bought the Morning Mine and many of the other producers in the area as well as a smelter in Everett, Washington. The mine was now a piece in the national financial structure, and was

THE ORIGINAL "GLORY HOLE" AT THE BUNKER HILL AND SULLIVAN MINE (N.D.).
In rare cases, ore was exposed on a hillside — as in this original open-cut operation at the Bunker Hill and Sullivan Mine. The two men in the upper left were double-jacking, and the man on the right in the center was single-jacking.

bought with Federal Mining and Smelting Company in 1905 by the American Smelting and Refining Company (ASARCO) as part of an attempt by its owners, the Guggenheim family of New York, to achieve their smelting monopoly.

Unlike the Morning Mine, which was bought by national financial trusts early in the twentieth century, the Hecla mine in Burke was owned by a series of smaller, more local investors during its first fifty years. Although the Hecla is one of the oldest continuously producing mines in the Coeur d'Alene district, the original claim was made not with the intention of mining but in order to secure space for railroad facilities and a townsite in the narrow Burke Canyon. The very first mining work on the original claim was done in a small mine called the Ore-or-no-go, partially owned by Colonel William Wallace, the founder of the town that bears his name.

Among the local investors was M. L. Martin, who bought five thousand shares at ten cents each in 1892 and then disappeared. The shares, represented by stock certificate #41, were carried on the books of the growing company, accumulating dividends for twenty-five years. Then in 1917, in a scene reminiscent of old-time melodramas, Mrs. Mary L. Humes of New York appeared with certificate #41, proved that she was formerly M. L. Martin, picked up a check for $26,500 in back dividends, and learned that the stock had a value of $40,000. Of all the stories of worthless penny stocks used for wallpaper or accumulating dust in attic trunks, those like M. L. Martin's fueled the dreams of small investors.

Large investors spent more of their time scheming against each other than dreaming of future wealth. A famous fight for control of the Hecla Mining Company took place just after the lucrative years of World War I. Fred Bradley, president of the Bunker Hill, proposed to James F. McCarthy, president and manager of the Hecla, that their two companies jointly purchase the Star mine adjacent to the Hecla. To consummate the deal, Bradley met secretly with McCarthy and other Hecla directors in

San Francisco in the early 1920s. They reached an agreement at a meeting from which McCarthy had excluded Hecla's largest shareholder, Sarah E. Smith, the widow of former Hecla president James R. "Hecla" Smith. Knowing that she would oppose the deal, he had intentionally left her out.

Sarah Smith was irate. The former head of a secretarial school in Chicago, she claimed that she had lent her late husband the money he used to develop the Hecla. Smith sued the Hecla management in two states and tried to take over the company at the annual shareholders' meeting. Although she had the very respectable help of Eugene Day of the Hercules Mine, she lost both cases and could muster only 16 percent of the ownership on her side at the annual meeting. She was dropped from the board of directors and the Hecla went ahead with what turned out to be a very profitable arrangement with Bunker Hill.

In contrast to those who made money from most of the major silver and lead mines in the Coeur d'Alene mining district, the people who discovered and profited by the fabulously rich vein of the Hercules mine were not professional mining people or wealthy financiers. They were hard-working small-business owners who worked the mine for twelve years using their spare time and spare cash, without finding paying ore. The Hercules is the most appealing of the success stories of the district because the people who made the discovery, and labored to make it pay, reaped extraordinary financial benefits from it. The strike was called the "Hercules" after the name on a box of DuPont blasting powder. It was discovered by Harry L. Day and Fred Harper in 1889 while climbing Gorge Gulch north of Burke after a forest fire.

When Day and Harper staked the claim, Day was a young retail clerk hoping to strike it rich from weekend prospecting. Fred Harper lost faith early on and sold his half share to his father-in-law, a local barber and part-time speculator, Charles "Dad" Reeves, who in turn sold shares to others in the area. Not until 1901 did Day know that he and his partners had a rich mine. During those early years,

HECLA MINE EXTERIOR, BURKE (1910).
Large stacks of timber were taken into the mines for supports and braces as fast as the ore was taken out. With the use of timber inside the mine and for surface buildings, the nearby hills were quickly stripped of their usable trees.

there was no return and they paid their assessments to keep the mine going with a combination of labor and cash. Then on June 2, 1901, Gus Paulsen, one of the partners, blasted through to what he described as a "cave of wire silver and lead carbonate." One assay at that time indicated 65 percent lead and 362.2 ounces of silver per ton of ore, or $269 per ton.

Day soon found out that getting the ore out of the mine was only part of the job. He then had to have the ore reduced in a mill and have the concentrate shipped, at the cheapest possible rates, to a smelter for the highest possible return. While he and his partners controlled the mine, large corporate trusts controlled the railroads and the smelters. The Hercules was one of the very few successful mines that remained independent. To do so, Day had to wage a continual fight for fair railroad rates, for railroad cars to take the ore, and for fair prices from the smelters.

During the First World War, silver and lead prices went up and so did production at the Hercules. This was the mine's heyday, with 900 miners working underground and with almost six million dollars' worth of ore taken out in 1917 alone. The life of the mine was short, from 1901 to 1924, and it was sweet. Over that period the total gross income from the Hercules was $43,000,000, at a time when miners were earning $3.50 a day. The people who were Day's partners in the Hercules were mostly common people who lived uncommon lives after they began to enjoy their share of the $19,000,000 in dividends that the Hercules paid out over its twenty-four-year lifetime.

The Day family as a group eventually acquired over one-half the shares, but those were split among five children. Paulsen not only discovered the vein of galena that made the Hercules famous and rich, but also was its largest single shareholder, with a little more than a quarter of its stock. He was a Danish-born dairyman who quit milking cows to work full time on the Hercules five years before he struck the ore vein. A quiet man of personal warmth, he used the $2,500,000 he received from the mine to invest in a utility company and to build Spokane's first steel-framed skyscraper. He died at the age of forty-nine of

HERCULES MINE OWNERS, SHORTLY AFTER DISCOVERING SILVER (1901).
A very satisfied group of amateur speculators were photographed by Barnard at Gorge Gulch, recording their moment of triumph after silver ore was discovered at the Hercules.

asthma aggravated by inhaling dust underground while he worked at the Hercules. He left a $3,900,000 estate and a twenty-four-room mansion in Spokane to his widow and three children.

When they were infants, Paulsen's children were the supposed target of a kidnapping plot organized by Harry Orchard, whose real name was Albert Horsley and who later became notorious as the murderer of ex-Governor Frank Steunenberg at Caldwell, Idaho, in 1905. Ironically, Orchard was also a one-time shareholder in the Hercules, having received a one-sixteenth interest in the Hercules from Dad Reeves in payment for hauling supplies to the mine. If Orchard had kept his Hercules shares in 1898, he would have been a millionaire. Instead, he became the most famous resident of the Idaho State Penitentiary. He had transferred his shares to Dan Cardoner, a Burke merchant, in payment for debts.

Harry Orchard was put into prison for murdering Steunenberg, and his confession was the primary evidence used by the prosecution to charge the leaders of the Western Federation of Miners with conspiracy in the murder. These leaders, all radical organizers in the miners' unions, were found innocent in a series of famous trials, the first of which pitted the future senator William Borah against Clarence Darrow, just then gaining recognition as a defender of progressive causes.

By far the most flamboyant of the Hercules people was May Arkwright Hutton, the wife of Levi "Al" Hutton, a Northern Pacific engineer. They bought 3/32 of the Hercules from Dad Reeves in 1897 for $505. May Hutton was a striking woman in both personality and size. Carrying her 225 pounds on a tall frame, she had a round and rosy face that well expressed both her joy and her indignation.

An orphan who started in the Coeur d'Alenes as a cook, Hutton first made her mark on public awareness when she wholeheartedly took the miners' side in the mining war of 1899. When the authorities arrested her husband for "assisting" the miners as the engineer of a hijacked train, she started an outraged campaign to free him. Her husband was soon released. The Hercules vein was discovered less

than two years later. With her income at last secure, Hutton became a social and political force in Wallace, entertained Theodore Roosevelt and Clarence Darrow, and unsuccessfully ran for the state legislature.

Mining has always been hot, rough, dirty, wet, and often dangerous work. At the turn of the century, it was physically exhausting labor done in dark, narrow passageways with a short supply of air, a great deal of dust, and few exits to the surface. The conditions, and especially the dust, limited the number of productive working years of the miner in the mines and reduced his life-span if he survived underground.

Considering the conditions, it has been difficult to put a price on the value of such work. For the first twenty years of Coeur d'Alene hard-rock mining, the miners were paid between $3.00 and $3.50 a day, working thirteen ten-hour shifts every two weeks, with the shift starting when they arrived at the work place inside the mine and with a day off on alternate Sundays. The miners' wages were higher than those paid for agricultural and other semi-skilled labor at that time, although a good case could be (and was) made that conditions for mining work required the higher wage. By the 1920s, the daily wages had risen to $5.50 and the shift had been reduced to eight hours, beginning at the tunnel entrance.

The miner's work clothes were simple and rough, suitable to the work underground. He wore leather boots, often hobnailed, to be changed for rubber ones if the mine was wet. His clothes were woolen "union" underwear, socks, a wool shirt, bib overalls, and a waterproof "jumper" (or slicker) that he took off when working the face of a drift. In the early years, he carried with him a dinner pail, candles, candle holder, and matches. In the 1910s the candles were replaced as the source of light by carbide headlamps.

The miners in the Coeur d'Alenes were a mixed bag of nationalities, representing the last remnants of the restless, independent men who roamed the frontier and the first generation of European immigrants searching for jobs in their new land. Only one-quarter of them were native-born Americans; the others were predominantly British, Italian, and Scandinavian. All foreign nationalities were represented except Orientals, who were still banned from the district by the miners who feared the competition of their cheap labor. The black was an exception in the predominantly white population.

Regardless of background, all who worked as hard-rock miners had the same ten-hour work day, day after day, with a Sunday off every other week. Their non-working life was not much more flexible. They woke at 5:30 A.M. to get dressed, eat breakfast, and have time to get to their stopes

in the mines by 7:30 A.M. to begin work. After working ten hours, traveling back and forth to the portal and on to their jobs inside the mines for three or four hours, sleeping eight hours, and eating for another one or two hours, the miners had little or no time left for recreation, family, or community activities.

Single men usually boarded with another miner's family or in large commercial boardinghouses called beaneries, often run by the company for which they worked. In the early years, most boardinghouses were dirty, damp, cold, and lousy. The food was often fly-ridden and the rooms

---

LEAD SILVER MINING COMPANY KITCHEN (JULY 23, 1910).

LEAD SILVER CO. MINE
TAKEN JULY 23, 1910.

smelly. The quarters were crowded and noisy, and privacy was unusual. However, the miners' major complaint about them was not their living conditions but the companies' requirement that they must live there, sometimes even if they were married. This issue came up repeatedly during the labor–management disputes of the 1890s.

Conditions had improved by 1907, when a boarding-house was built by the Snowstorm Mining Company near Mullan. The Idaho State Inspector of Mines said that the Snowstorm could "house 240 men as comfortably as any modern hotel." While there might be more than a little hyperbole in the inspector's remarks, the place was plastered inside, lighted with electricity, and heated by steam—all modern amenities for the time.

Neither the boardinghouse nor the Snowstorm Mining Company lasted long. The boardinghouse burned down several years after it was built, and the company exhausted its ore reserves of copper and silver by 1911. During its six years of existence, the only copper mine in the Coeur d'Alenes made more than one million dollars for its owners, the Greenoughs of Mullan.

The miners living in the boardinghouses ate a lot, if not well. At the Morning Boardinghouse, Fred Witts and his crew of eight helpers served 170 miners a total of 300 pounds of flour a day, 1,500 pounds of sugar a month, and 100 dozen eggs a week. The miners, of course, had to pay for all this. From a wage of about $100 a month, room and board would run from $35 up. The companies wanted to

Snowstorm Boardinghouse, Mullan (1910).
An unusually luxurious boarding-house for the miners at the Snowstorm Mine, this building had electric lighting and steam heat. Most boardinghouses were loosely fitted buildings heated by wood and lit by coal oil lamps.

have their workers living in the company boardinghouse not only because it made for a more settled, reliable labor force, but also because the company was making a profit from them. The manager of the Morning Mine wrote the owners in 1905 that they were making a profit of $2,500 a month from the boarders.

While company boardinghouses and stores were sometimes managed directly by the companies, often they were run by the superintendent of the mine as a source of personal gain. This was more common at isolated mines where pressure could be put on the miners to frequent the company's establishments, called "pluck-me" stores by the workers. In one instance cited, a suit of gum (or waterproof rubber) needed in the wet mines cost $19 at the company store in Burke and $11 on the open market in Butte. In 1911, requiring workers to shop exclusively at the company store was abolished by state law in Idaho, although the stores themselves continued in some areas.

Miners and mine owners alike, the people of the Coeur d'Alenes were unsophisticated but effective. All of them were more like the base rock from which the ore was taken than like the refined silver that the ore produced. If these men and women lacked subtlety, so does blasting rock miles under the ground. The personalities molded by such work were strong and direct. When they fought among themselves, as in the big mining wars at the end of the nineteenth century, their battles made history.

MINING WARS

⚜

THE EXCITEMENT generated by the gold rush into the Coeur d'Alene mining district was over by 1886. Fortunes were made after that time—but not by individual prospectors panning and sluicing gold from streambeds, and indeed not from gold at all. Rich deposits of silver and lead in the district were being mined profitably by heavily capitalized corporations employing hundreds of hard-rock miners.

The classless, anarchical society of the gold-rush boom towns was coalescing into recognizable groups aware of their own interests. Professional managers were running the deep-shaft mines for absentee owners, some of whom were financiers from the East and West coasts. The miners, a mixture of nationalities and origins, were usually unmarried men. Many were experienced veterans of Colorado and Montana mining camps. Early merchants and professional people in the towns of the district identified themselves with the miners who were their chief customers.

The miners were the first members of the community to join together for the advancement of their economic interests. A partially successful local strike was directed at the Bunker Hill and Sullivan Mine in 1887. However, not until 1890 were the unions secretly organized in all the major mines of the district. While wages were their first concern, the miners also banded together to change the conditions of their employment. They especially hated the companies' rules requiring them to live in company boardinghouses and buy at company stores. In addition, they wanted the mine owners to make the mines safer and thus reduce the large number of underground accidents, many of them fatal.

On January 1, 1891, the separate unions gathered together to form the Central Executive Committee of the Miners' Union of the Coeur d'Alenes. Their first major collective effort was not a strike but a hospital. The owners had been deducting $1 a month from the miners' wages, in return for which the companies provided medical care that the miners thought inadequate. The miners wanted to control their medical care and, through the new unions, contracted to build a miners' hospital at Wallace. They wanted the deducted dollar to go to their hospital instead of the company doctor.

When the unions did call a strike in 1891, they were successful in bringing all underground wages up to $3.50 a day, except at the Bunker Hill. In the meantime, while the miners enjoyed their first victory, the owners secretly organized the Mine Owner's Protective Association (MOA). Led by Victor Clement, the manager of the Bunker Hill mine, the MOA was formed to fight high railroad rates on the one hand and the unions on the other.

Thus the battle between capital and labor was joined. The conflict over wages for the men working underground was typical of the difference between the interests of the two sides. The owners wanted to realize economic benefit from new technology, in this case the introduction of machine drills in the mines. They could do so by lowering the wages of the unskilled underground workers, such as

muckers and shovelers, to $3 a day. The miners, however, wanted to keep the wages of all underground workers at $3.50 a day because they believed all workers were exposed to the same hazards.

The unions won the first round in August, 1891, when they forced Bunker Hill to go along with the other mines and pay a $3.50 uniform underground wage. Then, on New Year's Day of 1892, all of the mines were closed down by the owners, with the intent of forcing the railroads to lower shipping rates. Silver and lead prices were falling rapidly, and the owners could not afford the current rates. For the miners, it meant being put out of work in the

(Overleaf) FRISCO MINE AND MILL, GEM (1888).
Miners with their lunch pails and candles posed for a group portrait in front of the Frisco mill. Four years later, union miners blew up this mill.

(Right) FRISCO MILL, BEFORE 1892 EXPLOSION (N.D.).

FRISCO MILL AFTER EXPLOSION, JULY 11 1892

FRISCO MILL, AFTER 1892
EXPLOSION, GEM (1892).
*Barnard acted as photohistorian
when unusual events occurred in
the Coeur d'Alenes. He photographed the Frisco Mill after it
was dynamited by miners in the
mining war of 1892.*

middle of the North Idaho winter, without wages to buy fuel or food.

In March, the owners got their reduced railroad rates and announced that they would go back to their old differentiated wage scale underground when they reopened the mines on April 1. The unions refused to return to work, and the owners kept the mines closed until June 1. The MOA attempted to bring strikebreakers in from Missouri, Michigan, and other states; but the union men met trains, sometimes at the Idaho border, and forced the hated "scabs" to turn back. The MOA did succeed in running a secret train straight through to the Gem mines, where it unloaded strikebreakers.

The owners were prohibited by the state constitution from bringing armed men into Idaho without specific legislative permission, so they could not use armed guards on the trains. The two-year-old state government could offer little help to the owners because the Idaho militia was almost nonexistent. President Benjamin Harrison refused to send federal troops to help the owners unless there were a clear cause for action, such as violence.

The MOA was not defenseless, however. In addition to obtaining federal court injunctions prohibiting various union actions, such as interfering with the strikebreakers, the MOA hired a Pinkerton spy, Charles Siringo, to infiltrate the union ranks. So successful was Siringo that, under the name of Leon Allison, he quickly became the secretary of the Gem Miners' Union and thus privy to all of the union's plans and secrets. By means of a letter drop in St. Paul, Minnesota, he kept the owners fully informed of all union moves.

By the 4th of July, 1892, tension between the union men and the mine owners was very high. Arms had been brought into the district by both sides, and armed guards patrolled behind log barricades to protect nonunion miners at several of the larger mines in Burke Canyon. On July 7, word of the surrender the previous day of a force of Pinkerton detectives to workers at the Homestead steel plant in Pennsylvania reached the district. The union men were exultant.

TWENTY-SECOND U.S. INFANTRY AT WALLACE (1892). *Black federal troops, which the authorities used to impose martial law and control the unions, were stationed in the West because Congress did not want them east of the Mississippi.*

WALLACE, IDAHO, JULY 1892

During the weekend of July 10 and 11, armed union miners converged on the town of Gem on Canyon Creek, and in the hot, still July evening, nonunion miners were attacked and beaten on the streets of Gem and Burke. The fuse had been lit on this potentially explosive situation on Friday evening, when the unions discovered Leon Allison's real identity and occupation. Early Sunday morning, July 11, rifle fire began between the heavily barricaded Frisco mine, near Gem, and union miners in the surrounding hills. In midmorning, the miners sent an ore car full of dynamite down the incline toward the old Frisco mill, but it blew up short of its goal. Undeterred, they tried again an hour later, sending the dynamite down the sluice into the mill and blowing the four-story wooden structure into matchsticks.

The battle was short-lived. One nonunion worker died before the nonunion men and their guards surrendered under a white flag. The explosion at the Frisco was followed by the surrender of the nearby Gem mine, also under siege since early that morning. At Gem the fighting had been more fierce and the shooting more accurate: three men were killed on the union side, two on the owners' side.

Siringo hid at the Gem mine when the shooting started. As he told the story in his autobiography, *Riata and Spurs,* he escaped from his boardinghouse in Gem by sawing a hole in the floor of a back room. He dropped through the hole when the miners started banging on his door and crawled for half a block under the house and boardwalk, where union miners stood. From there he ran under the saloon to a creek, and on to the mine. When fighting got too hot at the mine, he slid out the back and hid out in the hills.

After the violence at the Gem mines, the rest of the district fell under armed union control without further violence. The unions paid special attention to the Bunker Hill and Sullivan Mine because of its past history of anti-union activity. There a union delegation, backed by some 500 armed miners in the hills around the mine, successfully convinced the owners to move all of their nonunion workers out of the district within forty-eight hours. With the valuable Bunker Hill concentrator under their control and

threatened with destruction, the union's demands were met. The nonunion miners were sent out on the next train west.

The victory of the union miners in the Coeur d'Alene mining district in July of 1892 was a limited one. For three days following their dynamiting of the Frisco mill and the gunfight at the Gem mine, union men held sway throughout the district. By July 12, however, both state and federal forces had already been set in motion to terminate union control.

The first countermeasures were taken by Governor Norman B. Willey, himself a mine owner. On July 12, he asked President Harrison for federal troops. That same day, Colonel William P. Carlin, commander of the federal troops at Fort Sherman at the city of Coeur d'Alene, received orders from the Department of War to move his troops to the "scene of the disturbance." He promptly loaded four companies of the Fourth Infantry on a steamboat bound for Harrison, where they spent the night.

That same night at Cataldo, at the head of navigation of the Coeur d'Alene River, an unknown number of unidentified men attacked and robbed groups of nonunion miners who had been forced by the unions to leave the district and who were waiting for the steamer leaving the next morning. Initial reports in the Spokane newspaper stated that a "massacre" had taken place, that the river was red with blood, and that the unions were responsible. No evidence of a massacre, or indeed of any deaths at all, at Cataldo, or of union involvement, was ever found.

Colonel J. F. Curtis, Inspector General of the embryonic Idaho National Guard, joined Carlin in Harrison as the personal representative of Governor Willey. He reported that 500 union men armed with Winchesters were waiting to contest Carlin's entrance into Wardner. Not surprisingly, Carlin and his 168 men advanced cautiously to Cataldo on July 13. Concern about the safety of the various troops under his command led Carlin to order Captain W. I. Sanborn to move Sanborn's three companies, which had advanced as far as Mullan from Fort Missoula, back to Missoula and then take the railroad around the area to join him on the west side of the mining district. The companies met on July 14.

Willey declared martial law in Shoshone County on July 13, thereby effectively bypassing the authority of any county officials who might be sympathetic to the unions. He appointed Colonel Carlin as the state authority in the county, with orders to arrest anyone who was involved in the Frisco explosion and the various armed confrontations.

Early on July 14, Colonel Carlin moved slowly forward up the Coeur d'Alene River and peacefully took possession of Wardner, Wallace, Burke, and Gem, watched, as he put it, by "several hundred idlers . . . lounging around the depot." That night, federal troops occupied all the towns of the mining district and set up their camps. Several county officials, such as Sheriff Richard A. Cunningham, Justices George A. Pettibone and W. H. Frazier, and Postmaster G. W. March of Mullan, were arrested and accused of aiding the unions. On behalf of Governor Willey, Colonel Curtis appointed Coroner Dr. W. S. Sims as sheriff in place of the arrested Cunningham. Sims and Curtis then proceeded to sweep each town, accompanied by federal troops, to arrest and (in the governor's words) "safely keep all persons known to have been engaged in acts of destruction to human life or property."

During the next few days, three more companies of the Fourth Infantry from Fort Spokane joined Carlin's force, as did 225 men of the Twenty-Second Infantry from Fort

---

FEDERAL TROOP ENCAMPMENT, WALLACE (1892).
The daily life of the federal troops was uneventful and rather boring for the few months they were at Wallace in 1892. Barnard climbed the hills west of town to photograph the encampment located near the city ice pond.

Keogh, Montana. In addition, 192 members of the Idaho National Guard arrived from southern Idaho. In all, 1,500 federal and state troops were brought in. With their help, state authorities arrested 600 men and put them in hastily constructed concentration camps or "bull pens" in Wallace and Wardner. In addition to guarding the stockade-like bull pens, which were used to hold prisoners, and to helping arrest union men and sympathizers, the federal troops were also used to guard the mines, which were reopened with scab labor.

State authorities soon came under pressure from two sides. On the one hand, conditions in the bull pens were primitive. With inadequate sanitation, poor bedding, and weak diet, complaints grew louder about the treatment of the union prisoners. On the other, the cost of keeping so many prisoners wore very quickly on the small treasury of the young state. The governor wanted the state to pull out of the district but was persuaded by the mine owners, with the support of Colonel Curtis, to maintain martial law until November 19, on the grounds that military occupation was necessary to prevent a recurrence of violence.

On July 29, the state succeeded in transferring custody of some of the prisoners to federal hands. The rest were released, with or without bond. Of the 600 who were arrested, 25 were cited for contempt for violation of the federal court injunction of May 28 prohibiting interference with nonunion miners. Fourteen were tried in federal court for conspiracy, and 42 were indicted in state court for murder.

In the contempt trial, thirteen were convicted by Judge James H. Beatty and sentenced to short jail terms in the Ada County jail in Boise. In the conspiracy trial, four were convicted by a jury and sentenced to terms of fifteen to twenty-five months in the federal House of Correction in Detroit. In the state's murder trial, all were freed by a Kootenai County jury.

By the end of March, 1893, none of the union men were in jail. Those convicted in the various courts had either served their short terms, been released, or had their convictions overturned by the United States Supreme Court.

The mining war of 1892 on the South Fork of the

Coeur d'Alene had one short battle, six fatalities, four months of martial law, and no victors. At its end, the owners were operating their mines on their own terms but had not broken the unions. On the contrary, the thirteen union members jailed in Boise came to the conclusion that they needed a larger and stronger organization with which to fight the influence and power of the mine owners.

Some of the imprisoned miners took their plans from the Ada County jail to an organizational meeting in Butte on May 15. Forty-three delegates from seventeen western mining camps convened there to found the Western Federation of Miners. For the next decade, the Federation was to be in the forefront of the union struggle against mining capitalists in the West, and then was to be one of the strongest pillars on which the Industrial Workers of the World was founded. In the beginning the Western Federation of Miners was a conservative organization, bent on obtaining higher wages, better working conditions, fewer Chinese in the camps, and the eradication of the company store.

As early as the spring of 1893, the mine owners were again in trouble. Though the unions had lost momentum, they were still effective, calling strikes that closed many of the mines. National activity affected the district as well. The Sherman Silver Purchase Act was repealed, ending federal price supports for silver. The panic of 1893, which swept the whole country into depression, lowered the price of silver by 25 percent and caused several local bank failures.

The owners were not in a financial position to pay $3.50 a day for all underground work, as the unions wanted. The mines opened and closed with the fluctuation of lead and silver prices throughout the year. On June 20, 1893, less than a year after the dynamiting of the old Frisco mill, Gem Miners' Union #11 astounded the district by striking the Frisco and Gem mines for the $3.50-a-day wage. But prices for silver began to improve and the railroads offered a two-dollar-per-ton reduction in freight charges in August. By the end of 1893, all of the mines, including the recalcitrant Bunker Hill and Sullivan, were paying the union wage.

The Bunker Hill lowered their wages again the next

year, providing yet another cause for ill feeling between it and the miners—a feeling that increased through the rest of the decade. Not only was the Bunker Hill the only major mine in the district to remain nonunion, but it began using Pinkerton detectives and other spies to purify its labor force of union sentiment. Reluctant to rely upon local enforcement for protection, the Bunker Hill organized its own Idaho National Guard unit among its nonunion workers and paid for it with company funds.

Popular opinion was on the side of the miners. A local coroner's jury in 1894 held Bunker Hill at fault in the death of three men and the injury of two others in a mine accident. The pro-union Populist Party swept the county elections that fall. Edward Boyce, soon to be the president of the Western Federation of Miners, was elected state senator, and Adam Aulbach, outspoken unionist editor of the *Coeur d'Alene Sun,* became a county commissioner.

While daily life in the Coeur d'Alene mining district settled down, the tension left from the 1892 war occasionally surfaced in violence. The miners were still bitter. On July 3, 1894, a group of forty masked men carrying rifles, their coats turned inside out, visited John Kneebone at his smithy at the Gem mine. The group was seeking revenge for Kneebone's testimony as a state witness against the union men in the 1892 trials. When Kneebone tried to escape, he was shot and killed. Four others were taken at the same time to the Montana border and told to stay out of Idaho. That same month, Bunker Hill guards thwarted an attempt made under the cover of darkness to blow up the mill.

There were other cases of people being run out of the district, and at least one man—Frederick D. Whitney— was killed in 1897 during a forced emigration. More significant, in light of later events, were a second unsuccessful attempt on May 10, 1896, to blow up the Bunker Hill mill and the successful theft by six armed and masked men of forty-six Springfield rifles and 10,000 rounds of ammunition from a makeshift Idaho Guard cache on May 13, 1897.

As the mine owners' prosperity increased toward the end of the century, so did the militancy of the unions.

Coeur d'Alene's own Edward Boyce was elected president of the Western Federation of Miners in 1896. He quickly built the organization into the strongest union force in the western United States, with hundreds of local unions and thousands of members. Affiliation in July of 1896 with the American Federation of Labor lasted less than a year; the Western Federation of Miners then broke away to follow its own more radical course.

In the spring of 1899, the Coeur d'Alene unions were as strong as the management of the Bunker Hill and Sullivan Mine was stubborn. In the seven years since the 1892 fight, every mine but the Bunker Hill had been unionized. Through a combination of persuasion and intimidation, the unions had obtained $3.50-a-day wages for all underground workers.

The Bunker Hill remained a constant irritation to the unions. If they could not force it to pay wages in line with the rest of the mines, how could they answer the arguments of the other mine owners, who maintained that the lower wages at the Bunker Hill gave that mine an unfair advantage in competing for investment capital and in producing profits? The unions had helped elect county officials, including the sheriff, who were friendly to their cause. They had strong locals and a solid regional federation. Yet as long as the Bunker Hill held out, they were not secure.

The Bunker Hill was doing more than holding out. The management of the company was dedicated to preventing the union from getting a foothold in their mines. For years, they had succeeded in ferreting out pro-union miners and firing them. The unions finally decided to unionize the mine secretly and by early April of 1899 they had carefully enrolled 250 Bunker Hill miners in the union.

On April 13, 1899, the union locals at Wardner met and decided to move openly for a union at the Bunker Hill. Edward Boyce was present to help formulate the union's requests for higher wages. The manager of the Bunker Hill,

Frederick Burbidge, at first refused but then acceded to the union's request upon discovering its strength. Yet at the same time that he agreed to raise all wages to $3.50 a day, Burbidge refused to recognize the union and demanded that all the union miners quit the mine. Several hundred quit after April 23, and others stayed on but refused to work. The tension increased.

The union put a guard on the mine's tramway and asked the mine to discharge all of its nonunion employees. Burbidge cabled Governor Frank Steunenberg on April 26, appealing for troops on the grounds that some miners were being prevented from working in his mine. The governor in turn asked Sheriff James D. Young of Shoshone County for information and received the reply that all was quiet and that there was "no armed mob."

While it is clear what happened next, it is not clear why it happened. The miners' unions met throughout the district early in the morning of April 29 and organized a mass movement of miners to Wardner Junction, where the Bunker Hill mill was located. Gathering momentum and numbers as they went, the miners took over the Northern Pacific morning train at Burke at 10 A.M. and commanded the engineer to move it down Burke Canyon, stopping to pick up miners along the way. Some of them were masked, some were armed, and many had white strips of cloth around their arms for identification.

Their intent became known when they forced Levi Hutton, the engineer, to back his train of three freight cars and one passenger coach up to the Frisco powder house, where they loaded sixty cases of fifty-pound boxes of dynamite onto the train. With this explosive cargo, the "dynamite express" (as it was later called) continued down Burke Canyon toward Wallace.

Near Wallace, where Canyon Creek runs into the South Fork of the Coeur d'Alene River, the train was stopped and 200 men who had walked down from Mullan joined their compatriots on the train. This group had reportedly stopped slightly north of Wallace and unearthed a large supply of rifles and ammunition, possibly the arms stolen from the Idaho National Guard several years earlier.

Word of the miners' approach spread rapidly through Wallace but did not get cabled to Wardner Junction because the wires had been cut. When the train reached Wallace, some of the miners got off and searched quickly for more guns and ammunition. While it was no secret that the miners, now numbering 800 or more, were going on to the Bunker Hill, it was unclear what they were intending to do there. In the engine's cab, Hutton was urged at gunpoint to switch his Northern Pacific train to Union Pacific tracks and take it down to Wardner Junction.

It was a bright spring day, and the train had much the appearance of an excursion as it slowly made its way down the South Fork canyon. The train was swarming with miners, many wearing their best clothes. Flushed with the anticipation of confronting their enemy, the union miners hung onto the passenger and freight cars in every fashion, some sitting on the roofs and others riding the coal car.

Word finally reached Wardner of the approaching union force, and the Bunker Hill management and its nonunion workers quickly evacuated the company buildings. The management was later ridiculed for the quite reasonable decision to hightail it out of town. Burbidge had no force with which to combat hundreds of determined miners. Resistance would have meant only a bloody, and losing, battle.

In the confusion following the arrival of the train at Wardner Junction, some of the men started shooting. Jack Smythe, a miner in the Frisco mine, was killed instantly, and James Cheyne, a worker at the Bunker Hill, was shot in the hip and died several days later in a hospital in Spokane. It was never proven who did the shooting, or why, but it was generally believed that these two were shot for being "traitors" or "scabs."

The shooting soon ceased, and the action focused on the new mill west of Wardner Junction that the Bunker Hill had completed the previous year at a cost, according to the mine owners, of $250,000. One of the most advanced lead and silver concentrators in the world, it was the pride of the company. It was also an attractive target for a group of embittered miners.

As the *Idaho State Tribune* described the scene in its next

issue May 3: "The work was planned and executed by men who received the training of a lifetime in the handling of dynamite." In a methodical and careful fashion, the miners placed the pilfered 3,000 pounds of dynamite in three locations under the mill.

At 2:26 P.M. the first explosion went off, followed immediately by the second and the third. The huge mill was blown to splinters in an enormous fireworks display that sent pieces of lumber and sections of machinery flying out over Kellogg, a mile away. A total silence followed, broken finally by the gunfire of the miners celebrating their handiwork.

The immediate aftermath was quiet and uneventful. The miners piled back on the train for the trip upriver to Wallace, where they dispersed to their homes. The mayor of Wallace had closed the saloons, although there was little rowdiness. The destruction of the mill had been enough excitement for everyone concerned.

In retrospect, the excursion to Wardner that day was a fateful one. The miners, in destroying the Bunker Hill mill, had also destroyed their union's strength. The forces of political authority and economic power could not ignore such a blatant exercise of union power. The counter-reaction that was already in motion that night would weaken unionism in the Coeur d'Alene mining district until well into the twentieth century.

When the news of the explosion reached the state capital in Boise the evening of April 29, Governor Steunenberg acted immediately. Although a former member of the typographical union himself, Steunenberg was convinced that the Western Federation of Miners was an anathema to the cause of good unionism and should be destroyed.

BUNKER HILL AND SULLIVAN MILL AFTER THE EXPLOSION (1899).
Barnard took a number of photographs of the damage. This close-up shows that metal did not survive much better than wood.

Steunenberg could not call up the Idaho National Guard because all of its members were already in service in the Spanish-American War in the Philippines. Therefore, by 11 P.M. that same evening, he sent President William McKinley a telegram requesting military assistance. McKinley concurred and ordered Brigadier General Henry Clay Merriam to go to the district from Denver to put down the "insurrection" that Steunenberg had declared in Shoshone County. In addition to asking McKinley for help, Steunenberg sent the state auditor, Bartlett Sinclair, to Wardner to investigate the situation. Shortly after his arrival at Wardner, Sinclair asked the governor to declare martial law in the district.

The forces opposing the unions could not have hoped for two men more suitable than Merriam and Sinclair to eradicate the influence of the miners' unions in the Coeur d'Alenes. Both acted with the dispatch and thoroughness that come from strong convictions. Together they were to bring the independent, individualistic, and radical hard-rock miners to heel.

Sinclair was the governor's personal representative on the scene, with authority to enforce martial law. He represented a governor who had been elected with overwhelming support from Shoshone County in 1896 and then re-elected without its support in 1898.

The first federal troops arrived in Wardner from Spokane on May 2: seventy-five black infantrymen from Company M of the Twenty-fourth Infantry Regiment, led by Captain Joseph C. Batchelor, Jr., who became famous later in the Philippines for leading a forced march against insurgents.

Although General Merriam did not arrive until a day later, the troops were under his orders as they sealed off the district by searching all trains leaving the area and removing anyone they thought suspicious. A systematic search of the whole district was soon under way. State deputies under Sinclair's leadership and supported by federal troops scoured the area and arrested all men who could not prove where they were on April 29. Since only 199 miners of the 1,148 employed in the mines at the time were at work that

day, the deputies had to arrest practically every miner in the area. At Burke, Gem, and Mullan, every man in town was arrested.

Mining in the district came to a halt for several months. The miners were willing to work. Indeed, in a display of either stunned naivete or subtle cunning, many of them showed up for work the day after the explosion. But soon the authorities had arrested and jailed so many miners that the mines could not be worked. This put some of the mine owners in the ironic position of wanting the authorities to back down and let their men out in order to get the mines working again.

When the combined force of state deputies and federal troops began arresting miners for complicity in the Bunker

Hill explosion, they had to develop a method of keeping them. The Shoshone County jail was much too small. The immediate solution was to put them in a large hay and grain warehouse and then shut the overflow up in empty railroad boxcars. The care of such a large number of prisoners would continue to be a drain on the limited treasury and personnel of the state of Idaho for the duration of their imprisonment.

Bartlett Sinclair pushed ahead with building a concentration camp, again popularly called a "bull pen," which contained shed-like bunkhouses enclosed within a pole stockade. By the third week of May the stockade was finished and approximately 500 incarcerated miners were transferred there. During the four months of their

existence, the bull pens became the focus of local and national outrage.

Legally, the miners were in limbo. Because martial law had been declared by the governor, the legal rights of everyone in the county—including the right of *habeas corpus* and the right to a speedy trial—had been suspended. The miners were kept in makeshift jails for weeks on end without knowing whether they would be charged or what they would be charged with. Of the 700 men who were held in the bull pen some time that summer, only 14 were eventually tried.

The prisoners' physical condition was precarious. The prisoners slept first on hay on the floor and then in bunks, covered with whatever bedding their families and friends

GENERAL VIEW OF THE BULL PEN, KELLOGG (1899). *The embryonic town of Kellogg was overwhelmed by the encampment and bull pen built by federal troops during the 1899 mining wars. The state authorities, supported by federal troops, lost no time in jailing most of the district's miners in the bull pen.*

brought them. Their rations cost fifty-six cents a day and were prepared, ironically, by the temporarily unemployed cook from the Bunker Hill and Sullivan mine. Three men died of various diseases while in the prison. Another went mad and drowned after throwing himself in the river while being escorted to the asylum.

One arrest that the state deputies were to regret was that of Levi Hutton, the engineer of the Northern Pacific train on that fateful April 29, whom the coroner's jury was later to call "the willing tool of the rioters." Levi Hutton was a quiet man but his wife, May Arkwright Hutton, went on a rampage when her husband was arrested. She wrote letters to any paper that would print them, called on any politician who was accessible, and continually harassed the military guards. Two weeks later her husband was released, but May Arkwright Hutton was just getting started. She went on to write *The Coeur d'Alenes: A Tale of the Modern Inquisition in Idaho,* a biting, sarcastic, slanderous condemnation of state authorities, federal troops, and mine owners. The main characters in her piece of barely distinguished "fiction" were easily identifiable. Her victims retaliated with their version of events called *Madame de Cowcount; or the Coeur d'Alene "Munchausen."*

The state authorities wasted no time in starting the legal prosecutions. By May 3, Bartlett Sinclair set up an inquest run by the coroner, Dr. Hugh France, the only county official sympathetic to the owners' position. France immediately started taking testimony concerning the deaths of the two men shot at Wardner on April 29. After three weeks of testimony, he turned over the evidence to a grand jury, which handed out 400 indictments in five days beginning June 12.

The authorities clearly could not try all 400 men, although they had already arrested more than that and were keeping them in the camps or bull pens, which were patrolled by federal troops at federal expense. The state could not afford that many trials and could not find a neutral jury in a county where the large majority of potential jurors were either in the bull pens or sympathetic to the detained miners.

The state developed a strategy of attacking the strength of the unions by discrediting their leaders. After searching the southern part of the county outside the mining district for nonunion jurors, they put Paul Corcoran, financial secretary of the Gem union and one of the most respected union leaders, on trial.

To help with the prosecution, the state authorities brought in from Boise the youthful William Borah, who made a name for himself when he demonstrated the truth of one of his witness's testimony by riding on top of a swaying freight train. Borah summed up for the prosecution and succeeded in getting Corcoran convicted of second-degree murder. While few believed that Corcoran actually did the deed and while it was never even proven that he was on the scene, he was convicted of conspiring to bring about the events that caused the killing.

Corcoran was sentenced to seventeen years in the state prison but was pardoned on August 14, 1901. The state's aim was not to keep the union leaders in prison for the rest of their lives but to demonstrate to the union members that their leaders were powerless.

Once Corcoran was convicted, the state called another jury to try more of the union leadership. But on August 28, 1899, the next eight men to be tried bribed one of the federal guards at the bull pen and escaped. By this time, the federal government wanted to withdraw its troops from the area and pressure was growing within the state to stop the prosecutions. The federal prosecutors stepped in at this juncture and convicted ten other miners of interfering with the United States mail because they had forced Hutton to take his train, with its sacks of mail, to Wardner. These men were sentenced to two years in San Quentin.

During the summer, the state authorities moved also to purge the county offices of any pro-union sentiment. By July 10, they obtained a court order removing Sheriff Young and the three county commissioners from office for malfeasance, charging them with a number of technical

----

INTERIOR OF THE BULL PEN, SHOWING BUNKS (1899).
The bull pen, used in 1892 and 1899, was a concentration camp for union miners held under martial law.

errors about liquor licenses and with failing to protect the
Bunker Hill on April 29.

Except for a few days at the beginning, the relationship
between Sinclair and his state deputies and Merriam and
his federal troops was to remain the same throughout the
latter's stay of over eleven months. Sinclair, acting on the
governor's authority, would make arrests, investigate the
mill's destruction, and destroy the power of the unions. The
federal troops provided the force to support Sinclair's
actions but did not formally initiate any action.

The military did get into trouble when they overstepped
these boundaries in their zeal. In one case, federal military
officers chased union members around Montana without
that state's authorization. In another case, the troops forced
miners who were on a sitdown strike to work.

An outcry arose from unions and populist organizations
throughout the country, attacking President McKinley for
using federal troops to repress the miners of the Coeur
d'Alenes. McKinley had, in fact, wanted to withdraw the
troops but kept them there in response to repeated pleas by
Governor Steunenberg and General Merriam that they
were necessary to prevent civil war.

As a result of the hue and cry, Congress held hearings
to investigate the charges of unconstitutional uses of the
military. On June 5, 1900, the Committee on Military
Affairs issued a report that exonerated the troops of any
misconduct and found that the bull pen was "a commodious
and under the circumstances, comfortable, prison." Seven
congressmen disagreed with this conclusion in a strongly
worded minority report.

Governor Steunenberg, however, was not exonerated.
At the turn of the century, Idaho's political situation was
chaotic. There were Republicans and Silver Republicans,
Populists and Democrats, and even a scattering of Prohibi-
tionists. Coalitions formed and dissolved, splitting the
popular vote three or four ways. In this context,
Steunenberg's actions in the Coeur d'Alenes did not find
favor. Some of the populace did not like his anti-union
policies, others did not appreciate the federal troops and
martial law, and almost all blamed him for the heavy cost

to the state treasury of the operation. The result was that
Steunenberg was shunned in the 1900 elections and subsequently moved back to Caldwell.

Although Steunenberg was ignored by Idaho's elec-
torate, he was vividly remembered by many unionists. On
the snowy evening of December 30, 1905, he opened the
gate through the white picket fence surrounding his yard in
Caldwell and was killed by a booby-trap dynamite bomb.
Harry Orchard confessed to placing the bomb and was convicted. The subsequent conspiracy trials exonerated
Western Federation of Miners officials Bill Haywood,
George Pettibone, and Charles H. Moyer of conspiracy.
The Haywood trial in Boise attracted the attention of the
whole country, was widely reported in the press, and pitted
Clarence Darrow against William Borah in one of the best-
known legal clashes of the time.

In planning their reaction to the union's destruction of
the Bunker Hill mill, the mine owners and their allies in the
state government wanted to avoid a recurrence of what had
happened seven years earlier in 1892. At that time, the power
of the unions was only curtailed by the presence of military
force, and when the troops left, the unions quickly regained
their strength and then grew more powerful. In 1899, the
mine owners wanted to eliminate the unions permanently.
They decided to accomplish this through a permit system
designed by the attorney for the Bunker Hill and based on a
system that the Bunker Hill had already used.

The proclamation establishing the system was issued on
May 8, 1899, by Bartlett Sinclair and approved by General
Merriam. It forbade the mine owners from employing any
men in their mines who had participated in the "riots of
April 29, 1899" or who refused to "deny or renounce membership in any society which has incited, encouraged, or
approved of said riots or other violations of public law"—
that is to say, any union member. The directive was ad-
dressed to the mine owners because, with the Bunker Hill
shut down, the new system was being introduced in mines
that had almost all been unionized before the explosion.

To be employed the miners had to have a permit, which

they could get only after swearing to an anti-union pledge before Dr. France, who had become Sinclair's assistant. The mine owners' effort to drive the unions from the Coeur d'Alene district succeeded. Of the 2,000 miners hired in the year following the explosion, only 130 had previously worked in the Coeur d'Alene district and only 99 had ever been members of a Western Federation of Miners affiliate.

At first glance, the permit system appeared to be illegal. Since March 6, 1893, an Idaho statute had forbidden any employer from denying employment to a person because he was a member of a union. It was not surprising, therefore, that the courts soon held Sinclair's system to be in violation of Idaho law. On appeal, however, the United States Supreme Court declared unconstitutional the 1893 act, which had originally been passed by a Democratic and Populist legislature in the aftermath of the 1892 mining war.

The permit system was the successful extension of the Bunker Hill's anti-union policies to cover the whole district and was unpopular among many people, including some

MEN DRILLING WITH WOODEN GUNS (1899).
The union miners incarcerated in the bull pen organized wooden-gun drills to pass the time (and probably alarm their military captors). Barnard would have needed special permission to get into the bull pen to take this picture.

who were not miners. The town merchants complained that the system chased out married men who, with their families, were good retail customers.

The state-supported permit system remained until January 11, 1901, when Idaho's new governor, Frank Hunt, discontinued the practice. The mine owners, however, did not want to drop such an effective weapon and continued it themselves by means of an employment bureau that they established in Wallace. This bureau, run by George T. Edmiston (called the "King" because of his power), remained the arbitrator of who was allowed to work in the Coeur d'Alene mines for the next forty-eight years.

The disappearance of the unions marked the end of an era. Just as the switch from gold to silver had meant the end of the individualistic, self-employed prospector, the introduction of the permit system meant the end of the fiercely independent union miner. Unable to work in the Coeur d'Alenes, union members scattered to mining camps throughout the West. Like so many sparks from a stirred-up campfire, some of them burned out and others started new fires.

DISPLAY OF IWW LITERATURE (1919).
In this photograph of confiscated IWW paraphernalia, the Industrial Workers of the World appears as more an administrative organization than a fighting force. After the 1899 mining war, the IWW found more success among the timbermen of northern Idaho than in the mines.

TOWN BEGINNINGS

⚜

THE FIRST towns—if they could be called that—of the Coeur d'Alenes were tent cities surrounding a few rough frame stores. They sprang up in the rush years of the 1880s and usually disappeared as fast as they arose. The few that survived did so either because they were residential communities for nearby mines or because their location on major transportation routes made them potential commercial centers.

Burke, Mace, Gem, and Wardner were all towns whose existence depended directly upon the mines. When the ore ran out or the towns were bypassed by transportation, they were abandoned. Wallace, on the other hand, was stable because of its location on the main transportation route through the central valley. It developed naturally into a commercial center than reflected the overall prosperity of the district.

Colonel W. R. Wallace, pioneer, prospector, and entrepreneur (but no true colonel), built his small log cabin in 1884 on high ground above the cedar swamp that became the town which bears his name. Wallace did not strike it rich in gold, but that did not discourage his belief that a town would be founded at the site of his encampment that would become what he called "a center of one of the richest mining sections of this continent."

Wallace split rails and fenced off from the public domain a forty-acre agricultural location he called Placer Center and paid for his location with Sioux scrip, which was originally issued members of the Sioux nation in return for confiscated lands. He and a few other settlers passed their first year there building bridges, trails, and a few primitive log cabins. These hand-hewn structures, without joists, ceilings, or interior walls, were cold and uncomfortable, but they did provide some protection through the first winter.

Placer Center was almost completely isolated during the winter, and Wallace was quoted later in the March 9, 1889, issue of the *Coeur d'Alene Sun* as knowing many "dark and gloomy days when none would take part in the townsite as a gift," when he had been called a "fool and a crank because I could see in the future a chance to build a prosperous town . . . ."

Lucy Wallace joined her husband in 1885, in time to suffer the privations of the second winter at Placer Center when supplies were limited and she did not see another woman's face for six months. Having exhausted their resources on improvements the first year, the Wallaces were refused credit for further development. "They called us crazy for locating a town in a place like that . . . . But Colonel Wallace was strong in his conviction . . . ," she recalled in a March 25, 1905, story in the *Spokesman-Review*.

In 1885, just as gold-mining opportunities were exhausted, the great lead-silver properties located on the South Fork began to produce enough high-grade ore to attract not only prospectors but also merchants, capitalists,

---

(Overleaf) WALLACE (1889).
As silver and lead properties started to produce, the town of Wallace, founded on one man's vision, became the commercial center of the Coeur d'Alenes. In 1888, Wallace had a hardware store, general store, post office, three-story hotel, stable, and enough board feet of timber from the sawmill to keep up with the building boom. A hill on the southeast corner of town provided Barnard with this view of Wallace—a perspective of the town that was repeated in Barnard Studio photographs many times over the years.

and railroad interests. Nearly all early merchants, including the first store owners Alexander D. McKinlay and Peter J. Holohan, owned silver claims. E. D. Carter saw the advantages of providing lodging for newly arrived fortune hunters and opened the town's first hotel in 1886.

Carter built a man-powered sawmill in 1887, added a lumber yard, and provided the boards for the emerging business district of Placer Center. More merchants moved in to "mine the miners." The first hardware store, J. R. Marks and Co., supplied the district with stoves, tin, copper, and sheet-metal work. Its owners were the registered agents of Giant Powder, whose dynamite was basic both to mining and to clearing cedar stumps from the swamp. E. A. Sherwin started a drugstore, offering among other things wallpaper, paints, oils, and cigars (five cents for fine, ten cents for finer, fifteen cents for finest).

Mrs. Wallace became the first postmistress, taking that opportunity to rename the town "Wallace." Stables, saloons, blacksmiths, and laundries soon followed. Businesses grew, multiplied, diversified, and changed hands as Wallace became established as a center of trade for the new mining district.

In 1887, the town of Wallace, population 500, was connected to the outside world by a narrow-gauge railroad. Colonel Wallace was on hand to deliver a welcoming speech, and the town's first newspaper, the *Wallace Free Press,* was on hand to record it.

Colonel Wallace's happy days in the town bearing his name were numbered. The scrip he used to locate his claim had been reported lost by the previous owner sometime before Wallace's patent was granted. Duplicate scrip had been issued that was subsequently sold to a third party who used it to locate a claim in North Dakota. Wallace was notified that he did not hold legal claim to the townsite, but convinced of his right to the land based upon his investment and improvements, he continued to sell deeds to lots and property.

In early 1889, the news of an unrelated Indian scrip land-ownership dispute in Montana reached Wallace and stirred the imagination of a few of its citizens. On the evening of February 19, 1889, a man walked to the corner of Cedar and Sixth streets at the very center of town and posted a notice claiming the lot. His action set off an epidemic of claim jumping as the people of Wallace realized that they did not hold legal title to the lots they had paid for. Men hurried from all over the district to claim a piece of Wallace, and home owners jumped their own claims to protect their investment with squatter's rights.

By morning, all unoccupied sites in Wallace had been claimed as Colonel Wallace stood by helplessly. "After I have proven the prophecy of five years ago, by my energy and work, they would rob me of what little I have left of the hardships and privations of pioneering," he complained bitterly in a letter to the editor of the *Coeur d'Alene Sun* dated March 9, 1889. Neither his eloquence nor his faith in the courts stopped the Secretary of the Interior from subsequently ruling against the town founder. The jumpers, including the majority of Wallace citizens, held their claims.

Wardner and Burke were established not because of the foresight of pioneers such as Colonel Wallace, but because of their proximity to the first silver mines of the district.

BURKE (1888).
Public sanitation was not a major concern in the early mining towns, as can be seen in Barnard's overview of the young town of Burke.

Wardner sprang up in the upper reaches of a short, narrow canyon off the South Fork of the Coeur d'Alene River, stimulated by the discovery of the Bunker Hill and Sullivan mines. Burke grew up northeast of Wallace along the banks of Canyon Creek, where the Tiger Mine had sent out the first shipment of silver and lead ore from the district. Their main streets consisted of wooden buildings crowded wall to wall into steep-sided, narrow canyons, with mine entrances perched on the slopes above. One visitor described Wardner's thin street as "one long argument," the loud conversations from one saloon merging into the next along the gauntlet of twenty-two drinking establishments lining both sides of the dirt street.

The canyon that held Burke is so deep that the sun could only reach the town for three hours a day in the winter. It is so narrow that the town's only street had to carry wagons, two railroads, and Canyon Creek when it overflowed its banks. S. D. Lemeux pulled the awnings on his grocery back to allow the daily freight through on the Northern Pacific tracks that ran down the middle of the street and straight through the center of the Tiger Hotel. The four-story hotel, originally built as the boarding house for the Tiger–Poorman mines, had 150 rooms and a "beanery" that served 1,200 meals a day. It burned down in a grease fire in 1896 but was rebuilt. The railroad tracks were built through the hotel in 1906, when Harry Day of the Hercules mine convinced the Northern Pacific to construct a spur track up to his loading platform below Gorge Gulch. The hotel covered the canyon floor that the railroad had to be built on. The Federal Mining and Smelting Company, which owned the Tiger–Poorman and its hotel, agreed to Day's request providing that "the portion of the hotel under which you pass is to be lined with sheet or corrugated iron as fire protection."

BURKE (1912).

The first shipment of silver and lead ore from the Coeur d'Alenes came from the Tiger Mine at Burke. The building in the background with the circular windows is the Tiger Hotel—famous for the railroad tracks that ran through it. This picture of Burke's unusual main street was probably taken for postcards.

Two of Wardner's more colorful characters came from the ranks of what newspapers of the time called "ladies of uncertain morals." "Irish Fan" was given to riding side-saddle on a white horse in a green velvet riding habit, a black derby perched on her flaming red hair. "Mormon Lil" won a piano in a contest for the most popular young lady in the community. Having one piano already in her establishment, she offered it to the local school but was rebuffed by the offended school board.

Periodic efforts to purify the mining towns of their "low life" met with little success. Wardner's police chief, Fred Decker, was not concerned with morality when he closed the city to gambling in 1906; gamblers were losing too much money and were leaving the town without paying their bills.

Though similar in social makeup and activities to each other and typical of mining boom towns in the West, Wardner and Burke differed markedly in the commitment of their miners to the union cause. Wardner, reflecting the strongly held attitudes of the owners of the Bunker Hill and Sullivan, remained nonunion throughout the period, while Burke was the center of union activity for the whole district.

Boom towns such as Wardner and Burke peaked before 1900 and gradually withered away. The mines became mechanized and needed fewer workers, who were able to live farther away because of better transportation. The Bunker Hill mine built a two-mile-long entrance tunnel out to the main South Fork valley in 1904, bypassing Wardner completely. Wooden buildings fell down from disuse or burned down in fires. With the miners gone, the towns died.

WARDNER (1907).
By the time this photograph was taken, Wardner was in decline.

WARDNER, TAKEN FROM THE LAST CHANCE MINE (N.D.).
Wardner was a true boom-and-bust silver town of which only a few foundations exist today. Barnard had a studio there for a short time but had the good sense to move to Wallace before Wardner's decline. The denuded hills resulted from fire and intense cutting.

ISOLATION

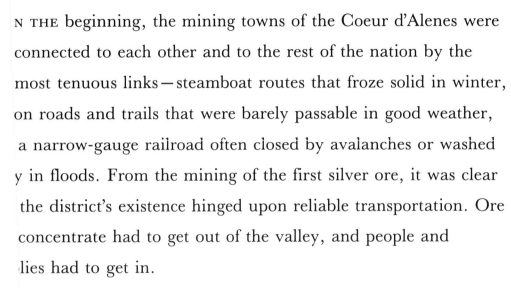

N THE beginning, the mining towns of the Coeur d'Alenes were connected to each other and to the rest of the nation by the most tenuous links—steamboat routes that froze solid in winter, on roads and trails that were barely passable in good weather, a narrow-gauge railroad often closed by avalanches or washed y in floods. From the mining of the first silver ore, it was clear the district's existence hinged upon reliable transportation. Ore concentrate had to get out of the valley, and people and lies had to get in.

While access to the Coeur d'Alenes was developed quickly to get supplies in and ore out, the area remained largely cut off from the rest of the country by its remoteness and severe winters. This isolation slowed development in the area and preserved the frontier character of its towns well into the twentieth century.

Much of the old Mullan Military Road was rebuilt in the late 1880s to connect the Coeur d'Alenes directly to established transcontinental railroad lines. But for the stampeders coming from the west in 1884–85, the fastest route to the district was overland to Coeur d'Alene City, then by steamboat to the Coeur d'Alene (Cataldo) Mission landing at the edge of the mining district.

Steamboat travel on Lake Coeur d'Alene and its tributaries started in 1880, when the military at Fort Sherman commissioned the *Amelia Wheaton*. Named after the commander's daughter, the boat brought in hay for the mules and firewood for the troops stationed at the fort.

Until the early 1890s, when the railroads took over, steamboats such as the *Coeur d'Alene, General Sherman,* and *Kootenai* played an integral role in transporting people and freight into and out of the district. A narrow-gauge railroad brought the ore from the mines to the mission landing, where it was loaded on steamers for the water trip to Coeur d'Alene City. There it was transferred to rail cars for the short run to the main line of the Northern Pacific. During this period, the steamship trade was so profitable that the Northern Pacific built a large, fast sternwheeler named the *Georgie Oakes* specifically for hauling ore. It was said that one run could make as much as $2,000 profit for the ship owners.

While improved rail traffic and the 1893 depression marked the end of steamboat ore-hauling on the lake, the boats continued to carry passengers. Then, in the late 1890s, the steamboat lines were revitalized by the need of the timber industry for transport to the huge virgin stands of white pine along the lake shore and up the St. Joe River drainage. In response to this new demand, the *Colfax,* the *Idaho,* and other steamboats were built between 1901 and 1903.

The *Colfax* was 100 feet long, propeller-driven, and rated to carry 250 passengers. Launched on July 25, 1902, she spent most of her time on the St. Joe River carrying supplies and people for the construction of the Milwaukee Railroad. A sign on her freight deck read: "No calked boots allowed on upper deck. Ask purser for slippers."

The owners of the *Colfax* faced stiff competition in 1903 when another company built the *Idaho,* a 147-foot side-wheeler that could carry 1,000 passengers with the unheard-of luxury of a dining room, wet bar, and 125 electric lights. In 1905 the *Idaho* had the misfortune of ramming and sinking another steamboat, the *Boneta,* on the St. Joe River in a confusion over right of way. No one was hurt, though the *Boneta* sank in three minutes.

(Overleaf) THE *COLFAX* (N.D.).
The steamboats of Lake Coeur d'Alene were popular as excursion boats after they were no longer economical for hauling ore or other goods. Barnard took this picture from a camp near the St. Joe River, where he went on holidays with his family.

(Below) THE *GEORGIE OAKES* (N.D.).
The "grande dame" herself on Lake Coeur d'Alene.

For local transport between smaller towns and from mine to town, people depended upon stagecoaches. The district's earliest stages carried miners from Mullan to the Morning Mine and back, moved gold bullion from the mills at Murray to the banks in Wallace, and delivered payrolls and the mail to the citizens of the Coeur d'Alenes.

Nova Scotia emigrant Alexander P. McRae started his livery, stage, and transfer business in Mullan in the early 1890s. For twenty-five years, his daily stages traveled the seven miles between Mullan and Wallace, crossing the meandering South Fork of the Coeur d'Alene River thirteen times.

In good weather, McRae drove a Yellowstone Wagon, a model designed for sightseeing by the famous New Hampshire wagon makers, the Concord Company. Its fringed top had roll-down flaps to keep sun, dust, and rain off the passengers. Its thoroughbrace suspension, consisting of a cradle of leather straps, let the passenger compartment

sway gently above the running gear and absorbed most jolts from the road. Three forward-facing seats and ample leg room gave passengers on this airy summer stage a relatively comfortable and reasonably safe ride.

Even the most modern rigs, in the hands of veteran drivers, encountered occasional problems. In June, 1908, a freight train passed the Mullan stage two miles from Wallace. The frightened horses bolted and several experienced passengers jumped for their lives from the runaway stage. But Joseph Herrmann of Wallace, who was riding next to the driver, was encumbered by a long overcoat and could not leap in time. He was thrown over the dashboard

---

McRae's stage (N.D.).
Sandy McRae held the reins of his four-horse team with both hands and controlled the carriage brakes with his foot in this picture taken near Barnard's studio at 4th and Cedar streets in Wallace. The location dates this picture sometime before 1907.

and dangled head down behind the horses, which had started to buck. Until the horses broke loose from the stage, Herrmann hung helplessly, each kick of the horses' hind legs narrowly missing his head. There is no record of whether Herrmann was refunded his $.50 fare for suffering the fright of his life aboard that Mullan stage.

Though stages and steamboats played important roles in connecting the Coeur d'Alenes to the outside world, railroads were the essential link. The first railroad was narrow gauge, built by D. C. Corbin's Coeur d'Alene Railway and Navigation Company with support from the Northern Pacific. Its track was laid up the twisting valley of the South Fork of the Coeur d'Alene River from the steamboat landing near the Coeur d'Alene Mission to Wardner Junction (later called Kellogg). The track was completed on Christmas Day, 1886.

While the Northern Pacific had its foot in the door of the mining district with Corbin's narrow gauge, the Union Pacific also was interested in the business of the new silver and lead mines. In 1886, it encouraged the formation of the Washington and Idaho Railway Company to connect the mines with the Oregon Railway and Navigation Company's main lines in the Palouse country of eastern Washington. By 1887, the UP had leased the OR&N, which in turn leased the W&IR in 1888.

The W&IR route ran northeast from Tekoa, Washington, below Lake Coeur d'Alene and then along the South Fork of the Coeur d'Alene River to Wardner and Wallace. After years of lobbying for federal permission to build across the Coeur d'Alene Indian Reservation and months of building track, Washington and Idaho Railway trains entered Wallace on December 1, 1888. The direct line effectively cut Corbin out of the competition and stimulated the Northern Pacific to build a standard-gauge branch line

ENGINEER P. SHEELEY STANDING BY U.P. ENGINE NO. 3513 (N.D.).
The driving wheels behind Engineer Sheeley were eighty-one inches high, the largest ever built for the Union Pacific. This locomotive was built for flatland passenger traffic and was out of its element in the mountains of the Coeur d'Alenes.

from Montana over Lookout Pass and into the Coeur d'Alene valley from the east. That line was completed December 23, 1890.

With railroads connecting the district to the main transcontinental lines, the first major obstacle to transporting ore from the mines was overcome. The problem of keeping those lines open, however, was never completely solved. It was virtually impossible to build railroad tracks so that they were out of the paths of avalanches and landslides. The canyons of the Coeur d'Alenes had narrow floors and steep sides. The canyon slopes near mines were stripped of trees for use as mining timbers, building material, and firewood, leaving little vegetation to anchor snow. Snowslides were common. Since little care was taken to avoid building in avalanche paths or traveling during times of obvious danger, people died fairly often and suddenly under huge piles of snow, ice, and debris along well-known avalanche paths.

The Black Bear snowslide of March 29, 1894, took place during a particularly severe winter, when northern Idaho was under twenty feet of snow in some places. Seven slides in all took place in Canyon Creek that day, including the one that swept through the small residential mining town of Black Bear. The slide, which occurred at nine in the morning, buried the entire Stefano Deiro family and two guests. The destruction also tore holes in mine flumes, cut off water to the electric power station that served Wallace, and threatened Wallace and other downstream towns with floods from dammed-up Canyon Creek.

It was not uncommon for track to remain buried for several weeks, forcing mines to close for lack of mining timber and supplies. It took hundreds of man-hours to clear a track and rebuild it after a snow slide, and once it was cleared and repaired, rotary snowplows were needed to keep it open.

When they first came west, the railroads tried a combination of wedge plows, brute force, and large labor crews to keep the trains running through the long winter from November to April. While the best technique for keeping the tracks clear was to maintain constant traffic on them,

(Right) BLACK BEAR SNOWSLIDE (MARCH 29, 1894).
The awesome power of nature was close to people in the Coeur d'Alenes. The search party is dwarfed by the snowslide that buried part of the town of Black Bear and the railroad tracks through Burke Canyon.

(Below) SNOWSLIDE, CANYON CREEK (FEBRUARY 3, 1890).
A large crew of men digging out a snowslide between Burke and Wallace gives an idea of snow-removal techniques before (and even after) the introduction of rotary snowplows.

that was impossible in early frontier days; there simply was not enough business. The first rotary snowplow was warmly welcomed by the railroads as the solution to their problem.

The basic rotary design has a square, open steel "catcher" in front that knifes into the snow, compresses it slightly, and holds it for the cutting wheel. The nine-foot-high cutting wheel inside of and behind the open square consists of a huge fan of blades that cuts and feeds the snow into the hopper behind it. From there, another much smaller fan blows the snow through a swivel nozzle on top that directs it 60 to 100 feet to either side of the locomotive. The rotary mechanism is mounted on the front of a car containing a large engine that powers the rotary blade and fan. The rotary unit must be pushed by locomotives at a pace of three or four miles an hour.

On occasion, even rotary plows found it tough going. Drifts two or three times as high as the rotary could slow it down to a snail's pace of sixty feet an hour. There was a danger of hitting debris inside a packed snowslide. The multi-ton rotary blade could cut through tree trunks and brush, but large boulders could tear it apart. Where there was a possibility of rocks in the snow, men went ahead with long poles to check.

While the Northern Pacific's cutoff from Missoula leading west into the Coeur d'Alene's was the most direct line into the mining district from the east, it was a pile of trouble in winter months. In 1903, the Northern Pacific's rotary snowplow broke down in heavy snowfall. Engineer George Morse was in charge of the rotary, which was coupled to a push engine followed by a passenger train and engine, a caboose, and another twelve-wheel push engine. The train was stalled in snow near Dorsey, and alternating train crews worked until shortly after four o'clock in the morning digging out the cars, section by section, fighting to

ROTARY SNOWPLOW AT THE
WATER TANK (1894).
*The big rotary snowplows were
essential to keeping the tracks
open in the winter. An avalanche
or heavy snowfall could bring all
transport in the mountains to a
halt until the train crews,
working around the clock, cleared
off the tracks.*

keep the train on its tracks in an attempt to make it back to Wallace. The crew succeeded in getting the train as far as the 839-foot-long "S" bridge that made a hairpin turn in a canyon over Willow Creek, eleven miles east of Wallace— the only bridge of its kind in the Northwest at that time. The push engine, the caboose, and part of the passenger car stood on the bridge where they would not be snowed under when the exhausted train crew retired to the caboose for a few hours of sleep.

At 7 A.M., a snowslide tore down the mountain gorge and swept away 150 feet of trestle at the upper end of the bridge, plunging the rear engine and caboose seventy-five feet into the creek bed. The engine was completely buried. The caboose, carrying seven crew members, stood on its end in splinters. A passenger coach carrying eight people

ROTARY SNOWPLOW ON THE S-BRIDGE (N.D.).
A rotary snowplow clears the tracks on the S-bridge on the route between Wallace and Saltese, Montana, where winter snows accumulated to a depth of thirty feet or more.

hung at a forty-five-degree angle, prevented from falling only by its coupling to the car ahead.

Jack Daly, a terrified passenger in the dangling coach, panicked and jumped through a broken window, falling into deep snow that saved his life. Other passengers frantically clung to the inside of the car and gingerly crawled to the front of the coach and through to the next car.

Two doctors were dispatched in a horse-drawn sleigh to tend to the badly battered survivors from the caboose and carry them back to Wallace hospitals, a trip that took eleven hours. All were in serious shock and none recalled how they got out of the wreckage—only that they had been unconscious for some time after the fall. No one was killed, a miracle attributed to a thirty-foot cushion of snow in the creek bed.

As long as the railroads were the primary link between the Coeur d'Alenes and the world outside, the railroad depot served as a forum of social activity and exchange. The Northern Pacific's depot at Wallace, a small, green-shingled, chateau-like building, was built of bricks salvaged from a hotel in Tacoma that was intended to be one of the grandest in the world.

During the 1880s and 1890s, the Northern Pacific was actively and competitively engaged in creating points of attraction along its lines to lure well-to-do tourists. With this in mind, plans were drawn up by the Northern Pacific and its subsidiary, the Tacoma Land Company, for a hotel that would rival the finest in the world—the Empress of Victoria, B.C., the Chateau Frontenac of Quebec City, the Shepherds of Cairo.

The seven-story Olympic Hotel was to be a replica of an old French castle at Chaumont. It was built of bricks made in China and carried as ballast on sailing ships chartered by the NP to bring tea to the United States. The Chinese bricks were light buff in color and twelve inches long, a style not found in this country.

The hotel was complete except for its interior in 1893, when a major banking crisis in England and fluctuations in the gold market precipitated an international stock-market panic that led to many bank failures in the United States.

The Northern Pacific, heavily in debt and largely dependent upon foreign capital, collapsed. The Olympic was boarded up and the NP went into receivership, to be revitalized later under the leadership of railroad magnates James J. Hill and J. P. Morgan.

In 1899, a mysterious fire started in the room of the Olympic Hotel where 80,000 shingles were stored. The fire gutted the structure. Without hope of rebuilding, the NP

S-BRIDGE WRECK (1903).
Two doctors, and perhaps the photographer, were dispatched in a horse-drawn sleigh to the site of this train wreck, which was caused by an avalanche in a tight, snowbound canyon.

The Northern Pacific depot at Wallace was a focal point of town activity and stands today as a romantic reminder of the heyday of railroads in the district. This picture was taken on film, not glass; judging by the size of the film used, it was probably taken after 1930. Other clues — including the crumbling stucco on the side of the depot — suggest that this is not an early Barnard Studio photograph.

decided to raze the upper floors of the hotel, salvage the bricks, and sell what remained of the structure to the city of Tacoma. The city eventually rebuilt the remains into Stadium High School. Salvaged Chinese bricks went into building five NP depots. In 1901, 15,000 Chinese bricks were sent to Wallace for its passenger station.

The depot at Wallace was designed by NP architects in Tacoma. Most NP depots were frame structures, rectangular, functional, and unadorned. Perhaps the romantic spirit that inspired the Olympic Hotel prompted the design of the Wallace depot with its tall, pointed roofs, rounded tower, and gently arched sashed windows.

The first floor was finished in Chinese brick. The second story and tower were half-timbered, faced with metal lathe, and finished in stucco. The first floor contained office space, agent's room, and ticket counter. For the sake of propriety, a separate ladies' waiting room (complete with bathroom) was partitioned from the general waiting room. The second floor contained six rooms: an agent's room, a roadmaster's room, a room for keeping records, and three extra rooms, one containing a bathroom. The third floor, in the tower, served as an attic.

As lines of communication and transportation were established between small Coeur d'Alene communities and the nation, some of the isolation in the Silver Valley was overcome. Yet when natural disaster struck, contact with the outside was severed, leaving the people of these communities with only themselves and their neighbors to rely upon.

Wallace, founded at the convergence of four ore-rich canyons, profited from commercial rewards such a central location was bound to bring. But it was also founded in a cedar swamp and was vulnerable to flash floods and seasonal overflows.

The citizens of Wallace knew that tailings from the ore mills dumped into Canyon Creek and the Coeur d'Alene River were filling channels with silt and sludge at the can-

yons' convergence at the east end of town. These deposits raised the riverbed. A bottleneck at this critical bend in the river directed the course of water straight through the heart of Wallace. The city appealed to upstream companies in early 1906 to quit dumping tailings during rainy seasons, and by May of that year the companies had drastically reduced the amount of coarse tailings run into the river. They had also agreed to pay, according to tonnage milled, the wages of men employed to shovel out beds, put in wing dams, and blast out tailings in an effort to straighten the river channel. But the cumulated effects of dumping were not undone. A pattern of emergency reaction instead of preventive measures developed.

Following a week of Pacific Northwest storms in November, 1906, the Coeur d'Alene River started to rise. By Tuesday, November 12, saloon keepers on the lower northeast end of Wallace were tending bar in galoshes, keeping an eye on the grey, swollen river that crept steadily through the floorboards. Men working for the mines cleared flumes and roads of fallen trees brought down by landslides. Railroad personnel waged a losing battle to repair washed-out track and telegraph wires. Wednesday evening, gusts of wind attended the continuous rain, uprooting huge cedars. As the crisis in Wallace grew, the Standard Mine sent 100 men and the Hecla called in its mill crew to dike the river above town, but it was too late. On Thursday morning, November 14, the city was under the worst flood in its history.

Wallace awoke Thursday morning to the roar of the river running several feet deep down the streets of the town's business district. Basements in the town were flooded, and stores of food and fuel, already in short supply that fall, were destroyed. Two hundred citizens fled their homes, and those who stood their ground worked frantically to save stores of provisions, furniture, and other personal possessions. The town was cut off from the rest of the world for a full day, with telephone and telegraph lines down. Evacuation to other towns seemed unlikely, as locomotive fires were doused when trains tried to pass over flooded track.

Added to the chaos were dangerous conditions created when sewers backed up, contaminating drinking water and threatening the town with typhoid. Another danger came to light on Friday as water began to recede, leaving one to four inches of highly toxic lead silt behind.

Floods were not the only natural calamity to beset the town of Wallace. As in so many other frontier communities, the town's frame construction made it vulnerable to fire. On July 29, 1890, almost all of the original buildings in Wallace burned to the ground, including the new studio occupied the year before by T. N. Barnard, who valued his loss at $1,000.

The economy was booming and the town was quickly rebuilt, this time much of it in brick. During the next decade, the city built up its fire-protection system, including excellent water lines, ample fire insurance, and a dedicated volunteer fire department.

In 1904, the department bought Combination Truck No. 1, built by the Seagraves Company of Columbus, Ohio. Truck No. 1 weighed two and a half tons and carried the latest in chemical fire-fighting equipment. The chemical apparatus consisted of a fifty-gallon tank carrying a mixture of bicarbonate of soda and water and a separate bottle of sulphuric acid. These were suspended behind the front wheels and were mixed at the scene of the fire to form carbonic-acid gas. According to the newspaper of the day, "no fire could live in the presence of the gas."

The extension ladders on the new truck could reach to the top of all buildings in Wallace except the Samuels Hotel. The longest was fifty feet and capable of reaching to the fourth story.

Wallace was a compact town, and the horses could usually get the equipment to the fire on time. Sometimes there were problems, as on July 4, 1904, when the tongue of the old hook-and-ladder truck came loose and the equipment overturned in front of the Wallace Hotel. The three firemen and Judge B. P. Potts of Mullan, on whom the wagon landed, were shaken up but not badly hurt. The problem was that the horses then bolted down Sixth Street, scattering men, women, and children in their path. Luckily the children who were run over by the horses escaped injury. The newspaper noted: "The fire was in a woodshed at Mayor Rossi's residence and was of no consequence."

No amount of new equipment could help Wallace escape from the fiery holocaust of 1910 that swept parts of three states; however, a heroic effort by the town saved thousands of lives and many homes and possessions. A lack of spring rains and drying winds from the southwest had parched Idaho and Montana. Hundreds of fires were started by lightning storms and railroad sparks, and by July 15, 3,000 recruits were employed as fire fighters in remote, often unmapped and trailless forests of north-central Idaho and western Montana. Supplies of axes, mattocks, shovels,

saws, buckets, and pots were rapidly exhausted at local hardware stores.

During July and the first weeks of August, the people of Wallace, sweltering uneasily beneath dust- and ash-filled skies, applied for fire insurance policies that were freely written, even as fist-sized splinters of fiery bark rained down upon the town from fires burning just six miles away. Residents still clung to the hope that rain would come, bringing relief to inflamed eyes and throats, sparing them the agony of abandoning their homes and livelihoods.

On August 8, President William Howard Taft ordered Army troops to help, but they did not have time to mobilize and reach the area. High winds blew up on August 10,

spawning hundreds of small fires from the large blazes and extending the fire lines dramatically. For the next ten days the fire fighters tried to reestablish control, but their efforts were overwhelmed by a gale on August 20 that united all the fires into a blistering conflagration that stretched from the Salmon River hundreds of miles north to the Canadian border. Eighty-five people were known to have died in Idaho, and 3,000,000 acres of timber burned. Smoke clouded the skies over the Great Plains and ash fell in Minnesota.

As the wind rose in the afternoon of the 20th, churning up towering black thunderheads, people in Wallace watched an orange glow in the southwest sky. Turbulent

WALLACE AFTER THE 1890 FIRE (JULY 27, 1890). *The rebuilding of Wallace began as the ruins were still smoking from the fire that leveled the town. Although Barnard lost his new studio in the fire, he obviously still had his camera and some negatives when he shot this panorama of the devastation.*

gases and cinders leaped rivers and surrounded valleys, pinning their inhabitants in low drainages. Most home-owners worked frantically to wet down their roofs and bury possessions. Others inexplicably hauled furniture into the streets. Many residents of Wallace spent the afternoon stuffing their worldly goods into suitcases.

The *Wallace Times* office was open for business at 9 P.M. that Saturday night as the first flames crested the ridge on the east side of town, swooped down the hillside, and engulfed the wooden building, leaving barely enough time for the staff to escape. Mayor Walter Hanson ordered Fire Chief Fred Kelly to ring the evacuation bell, signaling a stampede of panic-stricken women and children to relief trains headed for Spokane and Missoula. Terrified women

clutched screaming children as they scrambled with the sick and feeble for room in baggage cars, coaches, boxcars, and even flatbeds. All able-bodied men were ordered to stay behind to help save the town.

At 10 P.M., the east side of Wallace was cut off from the rest of the city. Buildings rocked on their frames, then exploded in the superheated atmosphere as the fire neared its peak. Volunteer fire fighters could not come closer than

FIRE DEPARTMENT HORSES, WALLACE (1907).
Chemical foam was introduced as part of the fire-fighting equipment while bicycles and horses still provided the only motive power.

WALLACE BEFORE THE 1910
FIRE (1910).

WALLACE AFTER THE 1910 FIRE
(1910).
*It was the Barnard Studio's
practice to take periodic
panoramic photographs of
Wallace from the same viewpoint
east of town. A comparison of
these two photographs taken by
Nellie Stockbridge before and after
the holocaust of 1910 shows
clearly how destructive that fire
was to the east end of Wallace.*

a quarter-mile to the flames without being knocked down by intense heat and blasts of fiery gases. The fire crew was powerless to stop a wave of fire that destroyed the town east of Seventh Street. Two thousand barrels of foaming suds poured into the street when the Sunset Brewery went up in flames.

Kelly and his volunteers worked through the night to save the rest of the central business district by wetting down buildings on Seventh Street. Two companies of black infantrymen from Fort Missoula policed the town to prevent looting. On Sunday morning, the fire started to burn itself out. One-third of Wallace had been destroyed.

Nellie Stockbridge, returning to Wallace three days after the blaze, found her studio intact and several glass negatives, which she had left on a gatepost in her haste to catch one of the last relief trains leaving Wallace, still in pristine condition. She was relieved to find the studio standing and the work of twenty years safe—especially as Barnard had lost so much to fire twenty years earlier. But she was later to look back with sadness to the time before the great fire. In a June 10, 1958, *North Idaho Press* story she is quoted as saying: "In those days before the fire, Wallace was a town of natural beauty, the trees in full growth surrounding it and the mining concealed by the gulches. . . . The homes of residents nestled on the hillsides made a picture not to be forgotten."

AFTER THE FIRE, WALLACE (1910).

Stockbridge took this picture on August 23 or 24 from the west side of Seventh Street — probably from one of the upper-story windows of the Samuels Hotel next door to the Barnard Building. In the foreground is the chimney of the St. Elmo Hotel; in the distance, across the river to the left, is the gutted Oregon Railroad and Navigation Company depot; and across the river from it stands what was left of the Pacific Hotel. The line of fire was held at Seventh Street, and the Barnard Studio was narrowly spared.

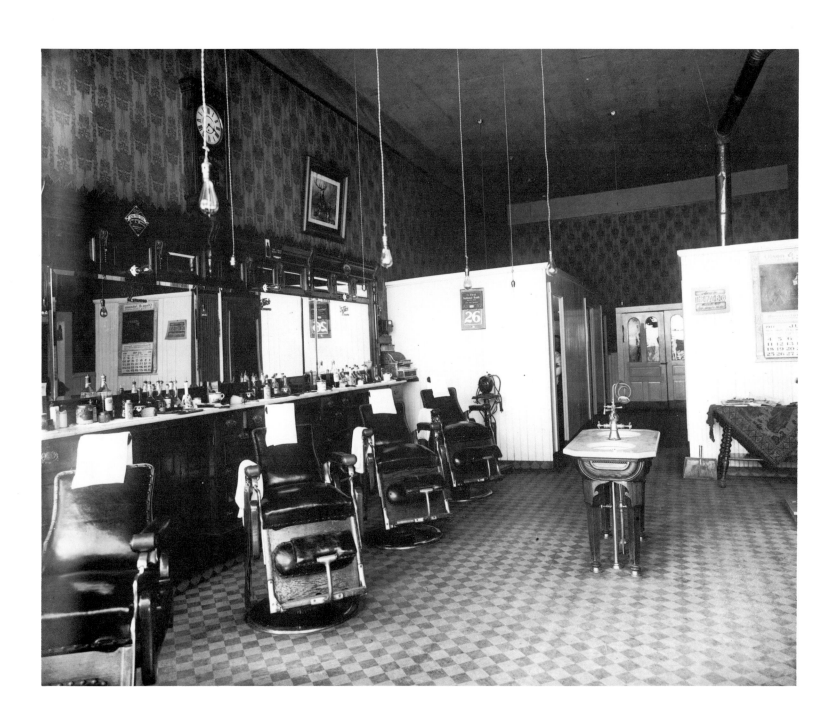

LOCAL ENTREPRENEURS

⚜

WALLACE grew as a community based on commerce. Between the fire of 1890 that leveled the town and World War I, it was transformed from a concentration of rough frame buildings into an established business center of brick. Wallace blossomed during the heyday of small-town life in turn-of-the-century America. Streets were paved, electricity installed, automobiles appeared, and ready-to-wear clothing was available to all.

During this transformation, Wallace's businesses retained a distinct quality that reflected its origins as a frontier mining town. This heavily masculine flavor was evident in the proliferation of bars, cigar stores, men's clothiers, and barbershops that dominated the commercial district. Slowly (and perhaps never completely) Wallace assumed the staid respectability and family atmosphere of a settled community. As a group separate from the miners and the mine owners, the merchants and local manufacturers helped create the basis for that community. Eventually beauty salons joined barbershops, movie theaters replaced dance halls, and men's clothing stores were supplanted by J. C. Penney.

Wallace's geographic isolation and mining-town character not only slowed down the transformation from frontier town to middle-class community but delayed — though it did not prevent — the impact on local business of the centralization of national economic activity. Local businessmen were at first rewarded for their entrepreneurial risk-taking; then competition from more efficient, centralized, national corporations closed many of them down. As with other small towns throughout America, mass production and improved transportation, allowing national firms to manufacture and deliver goods to Wallace more cheaply than local businesses could produce them, meant the demise of many of the local companies. The days of the local brewery, hometown cigar maker, specialized machine shop, and independent slaughterhouse occupy a relatively short time in Wallace's history.

With the exception of a few unusual women such as Nellie Stockbridge, men ran the businesses in Wallace. As in most towns, the barbershop was their frequent gathering place for gossip, political talk, and general socializing during the early part of the twentieth century.

In the 1890s, the OK Barber Shop was an informal mining exchange, a focus of fantasies, hopes, and disappointments in the town's favorite sport of mining speculation. Its proprietor, Charles H. "Dad" Reeves, was one of the most active participants, and one of the most successful. When his son-in-law, Fred Harper, traded his half interest in the Hercules Mine to Reeves in 1891 for some mines in British Columbia, there was nothing to distinguish the deal from any of the hundreds taking place in the barbershop about that time. It remained unremarkable until 1901, when the miners of the Hercules struck silver and the mine became the homegrown success story of the district, making

(Overleaf) THE OK BARBER SHOP, WALLACE (JUNE 26, 1911). *Whether he was there to take a bath, sell mining stock, or have his hair cut, a Wallace man found the barbershop a comforting and stimulating gathering place. The most elegant of ten barbershops in town, the OK had four oak, steel, and leather Koken barberchairs, a marble and oak washstand that provided hot water for shaves, and portable electric scissors. This photograph was taken on Monday, the traditional closing day for barbers.*

SIXTH STREET, WALLACE
(N.D.).
*The main business street of
Wallace after electricity but before
paved streets or automobiles. The
street sign on the left advertises
the nickelodeon on the corner. The
scarcity of women in the picture
indicates the predominantly male
involvement with the commerce of
the town.*

Reeves a very rich barber. In spite of having sold off all but one-sixteenth of the mine by that time, Reeves made over $600,000 from the Hercules during the next ten years, including the sale of his stock to Eleanor Day in 1911. Reeves enjoyed his money—until he lost it in a series of speculative investments in mining, lumber mills, and farms.

The OK Barber Shop had a large stove in the back that heated water for baths where men could wash themselves after a week, or even a month, of logging or mining. Most barbers arranged with a young boy to keep the stove stocked and bathtubs cleaned in exchange for the shoeshine concession. In 1911, a customer could get a bath, towel, and soap for four bits and a shave for a dime.

Like baths, laundries were a necessity in the early mining camps, and they were among the first cottage industries to grow up in the Coeur d'Alenes. Several different types of laundries developed to serve a growing and diversifying clientele, though the staple of the small laundries remained the "bachelor bundles" consisting mostly of men's starched detachable collars and cuffs popular in the early twentieth century. Few businesses in Wallace had their own laundry

BEER WAGON (N.D.).
A matched set of dappled grays pulled the Sunset Brewery wagon in this photograph taken at the heyday of the local brewery in America. Cases of bottled Pabst are piled behind barrels of local brew.

WALLACE LAUNDRY (N.D.).
Two kinds of horsepower teamed up to deliver starched cottons and linens to Wallace businesses and homes. This photograph is a typical example of Barnard Studio promotional commercial work.

facilities; most sent their linens, work rags, and kitchen laundry to a large commercial laundry where flatwork was washed in large metal revolving cylinders, belt-driven by steam. Fancywork was washed by hand. The Wallace Laundry grew out of the former Carter Hotel laundry, which used a wood-fueled boiler to provide steam and hot water to clean linens and towels for the hotel.

The first motorized fleet of laundry wagons was introduced at the Crown Laundry of Louisville, Kentucky, in 1913. But the industry continued to debate the reliability of the horse versus the automobile. For the Wallace Laundry, this question was still not settled in the winter of 1915,

when a team of Wallace Laundry horses drawing the laundry's sleigh through the snow-covered streets of Wallace bolted at the corner of Sixth and Cedar streets, pulling off the front runners and tipping over the rig. Three of the horses made off with the sleigh at a frothing gallop up Sixth Street where they were joined at the White and Bender warehouse by two teams pulling wagons filled with groceries. An American Express horse and its wagon got entangled in the stampede and, as all four rigs passed the Howes and King store, that establishment's delivery horse took off in pursuit. Though the horses were back in harness shortly after the fracas, with relatively little damage done to

WALLACE CIGAR COMPANY
(1917).
Small, local manufacturing operations, like this cigar factory in Wallace, were common in the beginning of the 1900s before the advent of national marketing and distribution. The success of cigarettes just prior to World War I drastically reduced the demand for cigars.

beast or man, the future, it seemed, lay with the automobile.

After a bath, a shave, and clean clothes, a man needed refreshment. In 1910, there were 1,500 breweries in the country, each making a unique beer for its local market. But the local brewery with its much-touted draft beer did not last long into the twentieth century. The newly developed refrigerator railroad boxcar meant that large breweries could sell their beer throughout the nation. If price-cutting competition from well-financed national breweries did not put the smaller breweries out of business, prohibition in Idaho in 1916 and in the nation in 1920 did.

The first brewery in Wallace was organized in 1889, but not until 1902 did Jacob Lockman build his Sunset Brewery on Hotel Street between Seventh and Eighth. He was a well-known figure in the area's flourishing beer and liquor trade and had become a local hero in Gem in 1893, when he arrived with a wagonload of beer after a flood had wiped out the town's entire supply. After the 1910 fire gutted Lockman's Sunset Brewery, sending thousands of gallons of suds into the streets, a new plant was built with an increased capacity of one hundred barrels a day.

The new brewery had only a few good years before Idahoans jumped the gun on the nation and voted the state dry in 1916. Sunset never recovered. Its owner tried to sell

COEUR D'ALENE IRONWORKS (1911).
This picture shows the manufacture of mill housing. The barrel-shaped housing was built to contain heavy iron balls that crushed ore as the cylindrical mill turned. The transparent appearance of the workman in the picture resulted from exposure of film to window light before the flash was fired, a technique used to compensate for dim lighting conditions.

soft drinks through the dry years but could not make a business of it. When Prohibition was lifted in 1933, the national breweries moved into the market vacuum with comparative ease. In 1934, there were 756 breweries operating in the United States, one-half of what had existed twenty-five years earlier.

With their locally brewed beer, men smoked locally rolled cigars. Most towns the size of Wallace had their own manufactured cigar brands. The Wallace Cigar Company was one of five local cigar factories in Wallace at one time. It was a labor-intensive operation; in 1907, it employed twenty-five hand-rollers. Brands such as "La Capella," "El Trinidad," and "Santa Clara" were made by blending and rolling domestic and imported tobacco leaves and hand-packing the final product.

Cigars, or "brown rolls," were superseded by "white rolls," or cigarettes, in 1909. Cigarettes could be smoked faster and were more appropriate for the faster pace of American life. They were produced in large factories using machines and were distributed on a national scale. Together, the growing popularity of cigarettes and their mass manufacture meant the end of most of the nation's 20,000 local cigar factories.

The fate of other local manufacturing concerns in Wallace was much the same as that of the Wallace Cigar Company. Too small to be able to afford to keep up with rapidly changing technology of the early twentieth century, local manufacturers lost out one by one. Coeur d'Alene companies that had been created to manufacture specialized equipment for the mines were also affected, although their financial connection to the mines enabled them to survive somewhat longer.

The local supply of mining equipment in the Coeur d'Alenes began when the first stampeder laid down part of his grubstake for a stove, candle holder, pick, and shovel. As mining went underground and mining techniques became more sophisticated, so did mining and milling equipment. In 1903 the Coeur d'Alene Iron Works at Wallace, consisting of a blacksmith shop, a machine shop, and a foundry, employed twenty-three workers who built

(Right) PUNCTURE-PROOF TIRE DEMONSTRATION, FRANK AND KRAMER GARAGE, WALLACE (N.D.).
Thirteen men and a dog add their weight to the back of the truck to demonstrate Lee's puncture-proof tires for the Barnard Studio camera.

(Below) PATENTED SIDE-DUMP ORE CAR, COEUR D'ALENE HARDWARE (1911).
Coeur d'Alene Hardware was a traditional machine shop that did custom work for the local mines but never successfully mass-produced locally designed items for a national market. Stockbridge may have taken this picture for a patent application.

YELLOWSTONE GARAGE (1926).
*Stockbridge came out on a wintry day to photograph a brand new van in
front of the local Dodge Bros. dealership.*

and repaired heavy mining equipment. The company was especially noted for its equipment designs. In the early 1900s James H. Taylor patented a side-dumping ore truck with self-oiling axle. Later the Ajax Patented Side Dump Mine Car, equipped with an ingenious lever mechanism that dumped ore and then restored the car to an upright position, was developed by the company.

As underground silver-mining methods evolved, local manufacturers of customized ore-cars, air-compression devices, and hoists faced stiff national competition. In addition, both the Coeur d'Alene Iron Works and its local competitor, the Coeur d'Alene Hardware Company, suffered business setbacks during a ten-year mining slump beginning in 1906, and both lost equipment and buildings in the devastating 1910 fire.

The only long-term hope for local mining equipment manufacturers was guaranteed sales to the local mines. The logical beneficiaries of such an arrangement were the mine owners. Eugene Day of the Hercules Mine and several other men with mining interests bought the Coeur d'Alene Iron Works and merged it with the Coeur d'Alene Hardware Company. The stockholders ordered their mines' purchasing agents to buy from the newly formed company, and the resulting combination of interest and influence effectively cut out any outside competition while it realized for the investors a 47-percent return on their investment in just two years.

Local retailers faced national competition as well and did not have the financial muscle and influence to stop the emerging twentieth-century retail phenomenon, the chain store. The opening of J. C. Penney's Golden Rule Store in Wallace on April 3, 1915, was ballyhooed in a full-page advertisement in the *Wallace Press-Times:* "men's heavy denim overalls, genuine indigo blue" for 98¢, "brassieres,

---

LINEMEN (N.D.).
A supervisor and his linemen struck a traditional pose for the photographer. Linemen were often transients in western towns, traveling along the line to wherever they were needed.

good ones" for 25¢. This Penney's store was the eighty-third in the Penney chain when it opened.

J. C. Penney Company was one of the first and most successful of large retail chains. Started in 1902 by James Cash Penney in the small town of Kemmerer, Wyoming, the company was based on a philosophy of no nonsense and hard work. Penney's policies of low prices, no discounts, and cash on the barrelhead attracted customers who were used to paying arbitrarily high prices for limited merchandise at company-controlled stores. In spite of some national anti-chain campaigns, the new retail system took hold, often with the support of local real estate developers.

T. N. Barnard was one such developer. In 1907 he built the Barnard Building in the 600 block of Cedar Street to house his studio, other shops, and apartments. The two-story beige brick building, designed by I. J. Galbraith of Spokane, is still standing with its metal cornice and brick parapet. Penney's Golden Rule Store opened in Barnard's building in 1915 and the Barnard Photographic Studio maintained its business there until Nellie Stockbridge's death in 1965.

While the Silver Valley was rich in minerals, its narrow

(Opposite) WALLACE MEAT COMPANY (N.D.).
The small-town photographer often took pictures of promotional displays created by local businesses for national manufacturers. Here the Wallace Meat Company is promoting Heinz products, for which Heinz gave specific discounts or provided free materials. Heinz was the first large food-products company in the United States to fund such local advertising.

(Right) COMBINATION WINDOW DISPLAY OF CANNED VEGE-TABLES (1938).
The owners of the Combination commissioned Stockbridge to photograph their display window for a promotional contest sponsored by Roundup corn.

canyons were useless for growing food. The district's need for produce stimulated a major agricultural industry in the nearby farmlands of eastern Washington. Most meat came to the district on the hoof and was butchered at the shop or restaurant where it was sold. Until the introduction of the refrigerated boxcar in 1890, the town butcher bought livestock, did his own slaughtering, made his own lard and sausage, and sold his meat over the counter. After 1890, grocery stores started selling meat shipped already processed from large national packing houses in the Midwest. At about the same time, city ordinances were passed prohibiting slaughter of livestock within the city limits, and the state passed health laws regulating the meat business.

The Brewer family, who took over the Wallace Meat Market in 1918, were able to fight the national trend by developing their own wholesale slaughterhouse a few miles up Nine Mile Creek, outside of town. They bought livestock from Montana and elsewhere, processed it, and provided beef and pork to the mining-company boarding houses, restaurants, and their own retail outlets. The Brewers also had a fish truck come every Wednesday from Seattle, providing the many Catholics in town with fish for Friday.

The Brewer family kept the Wallace Meat Market until after World War II, when the widespread use of refrigerator trucks finally made it uneconomical for them to compete with national meat distributors. By then, the butcher as well as the greengrocer and the bakery had been replaced by one-stop food shopping at the supermarket.

The centralization of American economic activity at first strengthened Wallace, making it the retail and commercial center of the district at the expense of the smaller towns, which lost the few stores they had as their custom came to Wallace. As this trend continued, local Wallace shopkeep-

ers lost out to larger regional cities and to national chains. Sixth Street would never again be as busy as in the halcyon days of the late 1890s, when independent shopkeepers competed for the miners' payroll in a frenzy of free enterprise.

JANTZEN SWIMSUIT DISPLAY, MORROW RETAIL STORE, WALLACE (CIRCA 1927). *One of Nellie Stockbridge's rare attempts at special-effect photography was this night-time promotional shot of a window display at the Morrow Retail Store. Note the Jantzen slogan: "The suit that changed bathing to swimming."*

A SETTLED COMMUNITY

✦

WALLACE changed slowly from the hurly-burly of rapid growth and single men to the calmness of stability and families. Churches, hospitals, and schools were built to take care of the needs of a settled community. A shorter work week in the mines meant more time for leisure and social activities. Local organizations supplemented the entertainment offered by traveling dramatic groups.

The beauty of the surrounding area made excursions into the countryside particularly attractive. One of the most popular trips was to the Coeur d'Alene Mission, located near the joining of the north and south forks of the Coeur d'Alene River. At the time of the mining boom in the district, the mission was over thirty years old and in disuse. It was already a historic relic and a haunting remainder of earlier activities of white men in the region.

The Catholic Church was one of the first of the white man's institutions to enter the area. During the 1820s and 1830s, individual trappers, often French-Canadian Catholics, and later the Hudson's Bay Company with Catholic Iroquois employees, developed contacts with the Flathead, Coeur d'Alene, and other Salish-speaking tribes. In 1841, Father Pierre DeSmet and other Jesuits visited the area to help establish a Catholic mission under Father Nicolas Point near what is now St. Maries on the St. Joe River. The site was often flooded, however, and the Jesuits decided to move the mission to a site above the Coeur d'Alene River.

In 1850, the Jesuits brought Father Antonio Ravalli from St. Mary's Mission in Montana to build the mission church. With the enthusiastic but intermittent help of three hundred or so Coeur d'Alene Indians, the missionaries spent fifteen years building with the only tools available: broadax, augur, pulleys, and ropes. Ravalli used a mix of European and French-Canadian methods of construction. The European method used a half-timber frame filled in with wattle and daub. The French-Canadian approach, called "post and sill," proved to be the more durable, and the church's wattle and daub was covered by clapboard in 1865 to stop disintegration.

The structural integrity of the church rested solely on design and careful craftsmanship. The beams were expertly joined by wooden pegs. The six large neoclassical columns supporting the porch roof were hand-planed to remarkable uniformity. The main altar at the far end of the church interior was separated from two smaller side altars by pillars. The church furnishings of Old World paintings, statues hand-carved by Ravalli himself, flowered cloth, painted wooden panels in the ceiling, and the fourteen Stations of the Cross on the walls gave the finished Church of the Sacred Heart a simple but majestic elegance. It undoubtedly helped focus the Coeur d'Alene tribe's loyalties on the mission and the Catholic Church.

Its days as solely a center of mission activity were short. Soon it became a way station for white trappers, soldiers, dignitaries, and pioneers as white immigration pushed the opening of Indian land to settlement and exploitation. In

---

(Overleaf) WALLACE–BURKE GUN CLUB (1894).
Nearly every man had a rifle and two fists in the frontier mining towns of the Coeur d'Alenes, a fact that may account for the immense popularity of gun clubs and boxing matches. The Wallace-Burke Gun Club dressed up in jackets and ties for a formal group portrait taken by Barnard in 1894.

1873, the United States government relocated the Coeur d'Alene reservation to the south, leaving the mission church outside the new boundaries. The fathers supported the move because it gave the tribe more arable land and the church a chance to build a tribal school. The new Church of the Sacred Heart was built near the town of DeSmet in 1881, while the old mission remained standing as Idaho's oldest and best-known human landmark.

There was no religious connection between the Jesuits' missionary activities among the Coeur d'Alene Indians and the newly arrived miners settling the district after the gold rush. The Catholic Church did, however, establish a major presence in the district early in its history by providing the administration and staffing of the miners' hospital in Wallace. The hospital was the first priority of the Coeur d'Alene Miners' Union, which entered into an agreement with the Sisters of Charity of Providence in 1891 to run the hospital.

The union had raised $2.50 from each of its 600 members to match a donation from the union treasury. A Missoula architect designed a four-story brick building with a mansard roof and belfry similar to a hospital in Missoula. The first floor had seven private rooms, parlors, a dispensary, a surgical suite, and an altar. More private rooms and wards took up the second and third floors. In a wing off the back were the kitchen and staff apartments. There were ten bathrooms, ten water closets, and an elevator powered by water brought by pipe a quarter of a mile from Spring Creek. The Wallace paper called the building style "just plain solid Western American . . . much thought for comfort, little for adornment," a description that can hardly be disputed. True to the founding purpose of the hospital, three of its first patients were miners—casualties of the bloody July, 1892, confrontation at Gem. The two union and one nonunion man were dead on arrival or shortly thereafter.

During the evacuation of Wallace in the 1910 fire, no arrangements had been made to transport hospital patients and personnel. While the hospital location seemed safe, it was not. Before the twenty-five people in the building could be rescued, the Bank Street bridge burned, cutting off the

THE OLD MISSION (1905).
Weatherbeaten and stripped of its interior furnishings, the Old Mission church overlooked a valley that fifty years earlier had been the heart of a thriving Jesuit Indian mission settlement. This favorite picnic spot atop a grassy hill was reached by boat from Coeur d'Alene or by dusty road. It is likely that the photographer took this picture on such a picnic excursion.

PROVIDENCE HOSPITAL (N.D.).

Providence Hospital was designed from blueprints of Saint Patrick's Hospital in Missoula, whose inspirational source, Mother Joseph, favored a rather austere, functional style. The building, captured by the photographer from some elevation and in the setting of the surrounding wooded hills, has a distinct rural charm.

PROVIDENCE HOSPITAL

main avenue of escape. The weak and despairing patients were finally helped onto a caboose and hauled to safety in Missoula by a Northern Pacific engine. Before the engine pulled away, a French-speaking novice, tiny Sister Joseph Antioch, ran back to the hospital to save three old patients forgotten in the basement. By the time she had gathered her three wards, the train had left. She and two of the stranded patients were taken to safety through the flying embers and gusts of hot air by the groundskeeper. The third patient stayed behind with Dr. F. Leo Quigley and a nurse to tend the burned, exhausted, and homeless who started to stream into the hospital during the next day. While the surrounding timber was reduced to ashes, the building was narrowly spared; the sisters later erected a statue of Jesus on the hospital's front lawn in tribute.

Hospitals were not used during the early part of the century as they are today. People did not go to hospitals to die of old age or to give birth. A report from Providence Hospital for 1907 shows 846 admittances. One hundred ten were victims of accidents, of which 82 were mine-related. Thirty-six patients died, including three from mining

SUNDAY SCHOOL PICNIC (1912).
A Sunday school class from the First Methodist Episcopal Church embarks for a picnic at the corner of 7th and Cedar streets, just a few paces from the Barnard Studio. Platform leaf springs under the wagon's box-shaped wooden frame gave the wagon the general name of spring-platform wagon. The presence of the single black child at a Wallace church picnic is unusual. He may be the same black child who was listed as attending Shoshone County schools during the pre-World War I years.

accidents, five from alcoholism, and four each from tuberculosis and pneumonia. There were twenty-three births, compared with the total of eleven births recorded between 1892 and 1905. The majority of patients in those early years were men, due to the dangerous working conditions in the mines and other industries requiring manual labor, and to the fact that men greatly outnumbered women in the Coeur d'Alenes.

Churches were important in social as well as civic and religious activities. One of the most popular entertainments was the traditional Sunday school picnic, which gave the adults some rest from their sixty-hour work week and the young ones a chance for games and gentle romancing. One such group, posed by Stockbridge at the corner of Seventh and Cedar streets on a summer day, recalls an unhurried, unhampered moment in the early twentieth century. Dressed in finery, ladies in summer hats, driver in Sunday coat and tie, the group paused in front of the firehouse for the picture.

The first civic projects of the new towns in the Coeur d'Alenes were schools. The district's earliest schools were log cabins where students of all ages huddled around woodburning stoves for a few months each year, learning without benefit of books or paper, often in a language that was not spoken at home. Schools grew up in every Coeur d'Alene community and were landmarks of civic pride and ownership. During the 1890s, when there was bitter struggle between management and labor over the district mines, some placed their faith in public schools to bolster democratic ideals they hoped would help soothe growing hatred and suspicion. Heralding the opening of the new public

---

(Overleaf) KINGSTON BOAT PARTY, COEUR D'ALENE RIVER (1897).
Improvements in dry-plate negatives, which required exposure time of only one or two seconds, made this casually posed but finely focused photograph possible. Only a playful kitten on the woman's lap on the left and a curious child in the boat on the right disturb the stillness of the pose.

MULLAN SCHOOL (1904).
T. N. Barnard set up his camera in schoolhouses of Shoshone County during the winter of 1903–04 to take pictures for an exhibit portraying the rise of public education in Idaho. The exhibit, which consisted of papers, maps, drawings, and handicrafts executed by county school children and documentary photographs taken by Barnard, was installed in the Education Building at the Louisiana Purchase Exposition at St. Louis in the summer of 1904. The exhibit was awarded seven medals of excellence by the exposition judges.

Wallace was originally built in wood, which was plentiful in the district. After the fire of 1890, when Wallace's business district was consumed in a matter of hours, much of the town was rebuilt in brick. The Wallace High School, built in 1892, dated from the construction boom that followed the devastating fire.

high school in Wallace in 1892, the principal was quoted in the *Coeur d'Alene Miner:*

> We are glad to announce to you that our school will open Monday morning, November 7 . . . . We believe that our public schools are the best institutions for making good citizens of the masses; that in them lies our greatest hope of solving the problem between labor and capital; of breaking down castes; of building up merit and dissipating all dangers from anarchy or jealousies existing between the different conditions of society . . . .

The two-story brick building was designed by W. A. Ritchie of Spokane and was constructed for $10,000. In a medley of Victorian elements, Ritchie included a modified mansard roof, Queen Anne decorative brickwork, Romanesque Revival brick arches, and—most ostentatious of all—an onion-shaped belfry. Above all, the high school was considered a place of culture and refinement. When the school was renovated in the early 1900s, the woodwork was stained and radiators were gilded. Along with statues of

Homer, Virgil, Milton, and Shakespeare were a four-foot replica of the Venus de Milo and reproductions of Millet and Rubens paintings.

In the early twentieth century the majority of Idaho's schools were still conducted by inexperienced teachers in one-room schoolhouses. Unlike the rural settings of schools in farm communities, the schoolhouses of the Coeur d'Alenes were located in towns, which often resisted the statewide attempt to consolidate school districts in an effort to upgrade equipment and teachers for the greatest number of students. People in small towns were reluctant to give up control and were proud of their ownership. Whereas students in the previous Mullan grammar school huddled around wood-burning stoves and worked without books and paper, the

BURKE HIGH SCHOOL'S GIRLS BASKETBALL TEAM (1908). *Bloomer-clad high school girls pose in front of a makeshift backdrop, suggesting that this picture was taken at Burke and not in the Barnard Studio. By 1908, nineteenth-century attitudes about what was proper for young ladies had relaxed to the point that sports for girls were actively encouraged in the public schools.*

BASEBALL TEAM (N.D.).
Baseball was a well-attended sport at the turn of the century, judging from the turnout at the grandstand at the northwest corner of River and 4th streets in Wallace. Pictured is the championship team from Kellogg.

BURKE MINERS' UNION NO. 10 TUG-OF-WAR TEAM (1906).
Once the largest and most radical local of the Coeur d'Alene Miners' Union, No. 10 in Burke had its social side too. In this picture the tug-of-war team is posed in front of the Shoshone County courthouse.

Mullan Public School completed in 1904 provided spacious steam-heated rooms, plate glass windows, modern ventilation, and a library for 120 students. While there was no compulsory education until 1909 in Idaho, Shoshone County could boast of a 90 percent enrollment in 1904.

Sports were such an important part of the schools' activities that there was an ongoing debate in the first decade of the twentieth century whether sports were not pushing education aside in some schools. The interest was not confined to boys' football and basketball; there were girls' basketball and gymnastics too.

Sports were just as popular in the community as in the schools. Participating in, or watching, the passionate sporting rivalries between different towns was a major entertainment. Baseball and boxing were favorites, stimulating strong loyalties and heavy betting.

Live stage entertainment was the first form of entertainment in the Coeur d'Alenes, but the era of vaudeville and other traveling shows came to an end after World War I. First the nickelodeon and then the silent film came into the theaters in Wallace that had previously featured magic shows, comedy routines, and melodramas. In the 1930s the movies became the dominant cultural influence in the country. Almost everyone went to the pictures. The Catholic Church and other groups concerned with public morality forced the industry in 1933 and 1934 to clean up its films and redirect its efforts to preserving what the moralists saw as the basic tenets of American culture. The studios did so, and made money. In 1938, when the total national population was 120 million people, there was an average of 80 million movie admissions each week.

Youngsters paid ten cents for their Saturday matinees, where they would see a feature, Buck Rogers serials, and cartoons. The matinees had more than just movies. The manager of Wallace's Grand Theatre, Fred Ketch, was a ventriloquist who performed with his dummy, Jerry J. Jerry. Ketch ran a Mickey Mouse club, organized various contests, and gave away prizes to the lucky kids. During the Depression, concessions enabled many theaters such as the Grand to survive.

GRAND THEATRE (1935). *During Hollywood's heyday in the 1930s, Saturday dime matinees attracted many small-town kids. No longer did the cowboy hero ride off into the sunset with his beloved horse: in* Bordertown, *Paul Muni had to deal with the likes of Bette Davis.*

NATIONAL PRIDE, LOCAL VICE

✦

THE PEOPLE of Wallace were swept along with the rest of the country at the turn of the century in a patriotism that supported America's emergence as a world power. They were not part of the American mainstream, however, in their pragmatic rejection of Victorian morality when it threatened the thriving local red-light district that provided an unusual source of civic funds.

American nationalism found as fertile ground in the Coeur d'Alenes as it did in the rest of the country. President Theodore Roosevelt embodied that new American aggressiveness in foreign affairs, and he received a warm reception in Wallace in the spring of 1903, when he stopped off there during his campaign tour for the presidency. He probably chose Wallace because of its political influence in Idaho, its importance as the hometown of Idaho's United States Senator Weldon Heyburn, and most of all its location on the railroad between Helena, Montana, and Spokane, Washington. Roosevelt was in the middle of a tour of the western states to talk about labor, trusts, national finances, and tariffs. He thoroughly enjoyed his two weeks in Yellowstone National Park but wrote that "I look forward with blank horror" to the political aspects of the tour. He arrived in Wallace early on Tuesday morning, May 26, 1903, on a special non-stop train from Walla Walla, Washington.

The visit was a major event in the town's history. The town had spent weeks in preparation and even tore down what the Spokane *Spokesman-Review* called "the unsightly porches which overhung the sidewalks." At a time when a man's suit cost $6, it was reported that the town spent $5,000 on flags, bunting, and other street decorations.

Ten thousand people from the surrounding area, twice the population of Wallace, turned out to greet the president and endured a steady drizzle to hear his short speech. The forty-five-year-old Republican was clearly popular — remarkable in a town that only four years earlier had been the scene of one of the most violent labor-versus-capital confrontations in American history.

Roosevelt might have been referring to this in his speech in the city park that morning when he said, "the worst foe to American citizenship, to American life, is the man who seeks to cause hatred and distrust between one body of Americans and another, and no matter to whom the appeal is made, whether to inflame section against section, creed against creed, or class against class."

Roosevelt's host in Wallace was Senator Heyburn, a mining lawyer who was elected over William Borah in 1903. Although fellow Republicans, the President and Heyburn were on the opposite sides of many issues, notably the question of the fate of publicly owned land in the West. Heyburn spent much of his senatorial career fighting to prevent federal forest reserves, and in 1907 he and Senator Charles W. Fulton of Oregon successfully pushed for legis-

lation prohibiting the formation of any more reserves in six Northwest and Rocky Mountain states. Roosevelt had the last word when he first administratively created sixteen million more acres of forest reserves in those states, and then signed the restrictive legislation into law (which also renamed the forest reserves as national forests).

On the day he was in Wallace, Roosevelt — successor to assassinated William McKinley and not yet elected president in his own right — received the telegraphed news that Senator Marcus Hanna of Ohio, his strongest rival for the 1904 Republican nomination, had quit the contest. The next day in Helena, Montana, Roosevelt wrote, "I am pleased at the outcome as it simplified things all around, for in my judgment Hanna was my only formidable opponent . . . ." Roosevelt went on to win the nomination, and then a full elected term as president.

As a long-time advocate of American assertiveness in foreign affairs, especially in the western hemisphere, Theodore Roosevelt would have approved of the enthusiastic reaction in Wallace in 1916 when Woodrow Wilson declared war on Mexico. Because the regular United States Army was small, on June 3, 1916, the United States Congress passed the National Defense Act authorizing President Wilson to use state militia to repel attacks on the country's borders. In a burst of patriotic fervor, Governor Moses Alexander of Idaho offered Wilson one thousand men and fifty officers and then called up the Second Idaho National Guard Regiment.

The cause of all the alarm and subsequent war hysteria was the Mexican guerrilla leader Pancho Villa, who had raided the border of the recently admitted state of New Mexico in March of 1916 and plundered the town of Columbus. Villa's activities led Wilson to send troops under General John J. Pershing in pursuit of Villa through the wastelands of northern Mexico.

Nineteen men from Wallace responded to Governor Alexander's call and were sent off south with Mayor Charles R. Mowery's words — "American citizens and soldiers have been slaughtered without cause. Their blood and lives cry out for retribution" — ringing in their ears. Of the

---

(Overleaf) WALLACE POLICE DEPARTMENT (N.D.).
Chief of Police J. W. McGinnis and four patrolmen of the Wallace Police Department line up for a photograph for Eagle's Day.

(Opposite) THEODORE ROOSEVELT IN WALLACE (MAY 26, 1903).
A steady drizzle did not dampen the welcome given President Theodore Roosevelt on his visit to Wallace, nor did it prevent this photograph from being taken from the Wallace Times building.

nineteen, six were miners, three clerks, three machinists or electricians, two teamsters, two cooks, and one a civil engineer. Two were unidentified. Harry Day, owner of the Hercules Mine, signed them up, and Lieutenant Hal Shadduck of the Idaho National Guard accepted their enlistments. Some 400 Wallace citizens sent them off on the train with hurrahs, flowers, and other gifts, though admonished by the newspaper not to bring "candies, cakes or pastries."

For the Idaho National Guard, the fight against the Mexicans was a non-war. The regiment moved to Nogales, Arizona, with 900 men but never entered Mexico, never fought, and was the only National Guard regiment left along the border when Guard units from other states went home several months later. One can guess that a professional army man like Pershing wanted little to do with quickly trained Guard recruits in the tough Mexican terrain. As it was, Pershing was asked to do too much with too little and eventually withdrew back across the border. The problems with Mexico were subsequently settled by negotiation.

Although the United States remained neutral during the first years of World War I, many of its citizens expressed their nationalism through the American National Red Cross. Woodrow Wilson's declaration of war against Germany on April 2, 1917, transformed the Red Cross from a weak, underfunded organization bound by charter to neutrality into a rallying point for citizens seeking to help the war effort.

Nothing short of a declaration of war would have mobilized so many citizens in so short a time to contribute to the cause. Mrs. Charles W. Beale, chairman of the local chapter, immediately secured the free use of a suite of rooms in the bank building and garnered the donation of linoleum for the floors, electric fixtures for the office, and sewing

machines. In an intense membership drive, the Shoshone County chapter enrolled 655 citizens as Red Cross members in the two days following the war declaration, and twice that number in the month following. "Comfy" kits containing toiletries, sewing kits, writing materials, and a novel were made up by the patriotic women of Wallace and sent to Boise for distribution to the Second Idaho Regiment.

SOLDIERS LEAVING FOR THE MEXICAN EXPEDITION, WALLACE (JUNE 22, 1916).
New recruits lined up with their recruiting officer for a picture taken by Stockbridge in front of the Barnard Studio.

While Wallace was typical of small-town America in its patriotism, it demonstrated its frontier mining-town heritage in its attitudes toward public vice. That heritage and Wallace's isolation in the mountains led to an unabashed and unrepentant acceptance of drinking, gambling and whoring, seen as commonplace elements of town life. This attitude continued long after the anarchistic boom days of the 1890s and even acquired a certain civic respectability. Their laissez faire attitude enabled the citizens of Wallace to raise funds for civic projects from taxes on bars, dance halls, gambling parlors, whorehouses, and other places of entertainment.

There was surprisingly little conflict in Wallace between frontier reality and American middle-class values concerning activities such as prostitution. Popular morality in Wallace held that prostitution kept together many respectable marriages, that Wallace madames gave generously to deserving charities, and that revenues from prostitution kept the city coffers filled and the streets paved. The lives of prostitutes were typically described as romantic, pas-

sionate, and pathetic. In fact, the "sporting life" very much restricted their behavior. Whores were strictly forbidden many activities that even the nineteenth-century woman took for granted. These restrictions limited where prostitutes could go and when they could be seen in public. In 1911, the *Spokesman–Review* reported that one Josie West was found guilty of registering at a Wallace city election in violation of a state law that disenfranchised inhabitants of houses of ill fame. She and her consort, Jack Madden, were each fined $200 and costs by Judge W. W. Woods.

The more successful prostitutes lived in "female boarding houses" while their less fortunate sisters solicited from "cribs," a string of cabins or hovels facing onto a back street or alley. The houses had parlors where drinks and perhaps conversation were preludes to sexual favors. A prostitute

could expect to part with most of the customer's fee for the privilege of practicing her trade, for some protection from violent customers, and for room and board. Should she survive disease, drink, drugs, and violence, there was little hope for her improving her lot through marriage.

The post-Civil War experiment of confining prostitution to defined parts of the city, called restricted districts, lost much of its popular support in the later part of the century, when local moral outrage would periodically close the restricted districts and their associated vices. On one such

---

AMERICAN WAR MOTHERS AT THE STONE RESIDENCE (1927).
War Mothers of Wallace kept candles burning in their windows for American servicemen and women.

occasion in 1903, Wallace's mayor ordered the police chief to evict all women of questionable character from the town, having closed down all gambling the night before and having set an example by turning the slot machine at his cigar store to the wall. Off the record, however, the mayor accused various officials of attempting to make a Sunday school out of Wallace.

Later, in 1917, the U.S. War Department got involved and requested that the area be closed. Federal law prohibited restricted areas within a specified distance of military camps, and Wallace's district was well within the prohibited zone. A U.S. Army lieutenant, in an address at the Methodist church reported in the *Wallace Press-Times,* exhorted Wallace citizens to "think of the sons, brothers, husbands and fathers who are allowed to contribute to the school fund through this source of revenue! Think of educating your children with tainted money!" Pleading that soldiers are useless if debilitated by venereal disease, the lieutenant cited the fall of Rome as an example of what Wallace could expect if it let prostitution thrive in its midst. Once again, the district was closed.

The restricted district in Wallace was located in a triangle between Cedar Street, Fifth Street, and the river, and contained the full range of businesses catering to men's baser desires: bars, saloons, dance halls, gambling and card rooms, variety theaters, and brothels. One of the earliest of these types of business was the hurdy-gurdy, a crude form of dance hall that blossomed briefly in the gold-rush camps but died out as camps became towns. In the towns, a marginally more refined dance hall became popular. There, young women would sell dances to clients and march them to the bar between numbers for the mandatory one-dollar drink. The profit was made off the alcohol; the women were not necessarily prostitutes.

The variety or bawdy theater, of which Wallace had several, was a combination of saloon and vaudeville. Shadow plays, traveling actresses, singers, and dancers performed for predominantly, though not exclusively, male audiences. Between shows, the performers or house girls would sell drinks to the audience. It was no secret that for a price customers could enjoy the sexual favors of certain performers in the privacy of curtained balcony boxes.

Variety theaters suffered the same fate as hurdy-gurdies and disappeared from the western scene, the victims of crusading moralists, campaigning politicians, and more novel forms of entertainment, such as the nickelodeon. In 1911, the *Spokesman-Review* reported the closing of the Arcade Theatre in Wallace:

> With the closing of the bars in the Arcade Theatre today, one of the last of the west's notorious dance halls passed into history. Today's action came as a result of the commisioners refusal to again grant the liquor license of Dan McInnis, the proprietor.
>
> For years the sentiment which crushed the Coeur d'Alene theatre in Spokane and similar institutions in other towns has been growing in Wallace. At the recent city campaign this dance hall was made an issue. Both sides promised to curb it if put in power . . . .
>
> Like the dance halls which have gone before it, the Arcade was a combination of women, wine and song. It consisted of its bars, its dance floor and stage and its curtained boxes.
>
> Beer at $1 a bottle has furnished the major part of the profits.
>
> . . . McInnis, the proprietor, has not yet announced his plans for the future, but with its liquor profits gone, it is a foregone conclusion that the theatre will not continue in its present form.

The last vestige of the early frontier hurdy-gurdies, dance halls, and variety theaters survived in the form of two- and three-man bands that played dance music and popular sentimental tunes in saloons. A two-man band playing at the Montana Bar had a repertoire including the 1912 hit "Gee But It's Great to Meet a Friend From Your Home Town." A sign asked, "Are You Ever Going to Buy a Drink?" and from the ceiling and walls hung pin-up postcards, a lady's corset, paper flowers, and other tokens of cheap sentiment.

TWO-MAN BAND, MONTANA SALOON (N.D.).
Barnard and Stockbridge routinely took photographs inside commercial establishments at the owners' request, but this photograph is unusual in both its subject and its locale. Poorly lit saloons were not a common setting for Barnard group portraits, but then the studio was not commonly called upon to take pictures of local entertainers on location.

Wallace's wide-open nightlife could not have existed without the acquiescence of its politicians and leading citizens. Herman J. Rossi was both, and his political career was to intermingle with Wallace history over forty years. He was an extraordinary personality who was four times mayor of Wallace, a state representative, a regent of the University of Idaho, chairman of the Idaho Board of Education, president of the Wallace Board of Trade, lieutenant colonel in the Idaho National Guard, and a successful insurance executive and mine owner. His respectable career becomes exceptional in the context of his having, during this same period, publicly shot and killed a man, for which he was found not guilty by reason of temporary insanity, and his later being convicted of large-scale violations of the federal Prohibition (Volstead) Act.

As were many other self-made men of this time, Rossi was a strong-willed individual. This and his hot temper got him into trouble in 1916. His second wife, who was fifteen years younger than he, had a drinking problem that worsened during their marriage. Although attempts were made, there seems to have been no cure for her alcoholism. On June 30, 1916, Rossi returned from a Republican state platform meeting in Boise to find his wife drunk in her bedroom and the maid full of tales of debauchery. Rossi stormed downtown to the Samuels Hotel, where he assaulted his wife's supposed lover in the lobby and then shot him in the back as he tried to run away. Rossi went to his attorney's office where he was arrested, taken to the police station, booked, and released on $10,000 bail put up by some of the town's most prominent citizens.

Three and a half months later, Rossi was unanimously found not guilty by reason of temporary insanity by a hometown jury after less than twenty minutes' deliberation. The judge, W. W. Woods, was a fellow Elk and Mason and a co-director with Rossi in the Amazon Dixie Mine. There was never any question that Rossi shot the man, but there was a general community feeling that he had been grievously wronged and had made just retribution. Demonstrating their love for sensation and a flair for paradox, the people of Wallace turned out in such large numbers for the

funeral of the victim that it was the best-attended event held up to that time in Wallace.

Fully exonerated, Rossi continued his energetic career. The next year, he married Bernice Johnson of Boise in May and in July was organizing a citizens' alliance in Wallace to collect Red Cross soldiers' relief funds and to warn German sympathizers to leave town.

The story of Rossi's wife's alcoholism would have made fit propaganda for the very active proponents of Prohibition, who on January 1, 1916, succeeded in making Idaho a dry state. Ironically, Rossi was heavily involved in keeping Shoshone as "wet" as possible, and eventually was convicted for his involvement.

At the height of Idaho's anti-liquor sentiment in 1916, Shoshone County was less enthusiastic about Prohibition than was the rest of the state. Miners have traditionally been hard drinkers, and the miners of the Coeur d'Alenes were no exception. Evasion of state and then federal Prohibition became common, and even blatant, in the district for the next seventeen years. During the first few years of Idaho state prohibition, the mining district received its alcohol by a weekly train from Montana, which was still wet, and from occasional pack trains that smuggled liquor in across the mountains. It was clear that the Shoshone County sheriffs were expected not to enforce the law, under pain of popular retaliation.

Because of his involvement in city politics, Rossi was aware that liquor licenses, upon which the city and the county depended for much of their revenue, were transformed into "soft drink" licenses at the time of state prohibition in 1916. When he was elected mayor for the third time in 1929, Rossi became an active participant in this long-standing, large-scale, and quite open defiance of state and federal laws.

UNIDENTIFIED PROSTITUTE (N.D.).
Stockbridge was hired by the Wallace Police Department to take the police photographs (above) of prostitutes during World War II. Occasionally the woman would ask her to take an additional photograph (below) to send to friends and relatives.

The county's obvious evasion of the law did not go un-challenged. On August 14, 1929, federal and state agents coordinated arrests throughout the county, arresting forty offenders and confiscating 600 gallons of liquor in their attack on what they called "the North Idaho Whiskey Rebellion." Although this taxed the capacity of the county jail, it was just the beginning. Before the liquor agents were finished, federal undercover agents had arrested almost 200 county residents, including Shoshone County Sheriff R. E. Weniger, the deputy sheriff, the county assessor, and city and police officials from both Mullan and Wallace, including Mayor Rossi.

The charges left little doubt that there was wholesale and concerted evasion of the Volstead Act in Shoshone County. The county and its principal cities had openly licensed saloons at $25 a month under the thin disguise of soft drink parlors. Local officials maintained that such revenues went to legitimate city projects, in line with the conventional Shoshone County belief that taxation of "vice" was essential to funding local government. While the morality of the system was debatable, its effectiveness was not. In 1911, for example, the sheriff reported clearing $100,000 in license revenue for the year. As State Representative Adam Aulbach argued in a speech against the "drys" in the Idaho House in 1905, prohibition invited "commercial suicide" and liquor-license revenue was "indispensable and irreplaceable."

But in 1929 the federal courts did not agree. Very few

(Right) Elks Boxing Team (1902).
Two boxers from the Elks Club and their coach pose before a Victorian backdrop in the Barnard Studio. Herman Rossi is the boxer on the left.

(Opposite) "Wallpaper Store" (N.D.).
The purpose of this photograph (taken sometime in the 1920s) was to promote the Coeur d'Alene Fruit Store, owned by the Armani Brothers, and to show off the business's new delivery truck. But to a generation of Wallace men, "a visit to the paint store (or wallpaper store)" meant a joyride through Wallace's restricted district, where legitimate businesses and brothels often stood side by side.

of those arrested were acquitted. Sheriff Weniger was sentenced to two years in the federal penitentiary and Rossi to a year and a half. The latter never served his sentence but did resign as mayor.

In 1935, Herman Rossi was elected to his fourth term as mayor of Wallace, a true representative of the people of the town. Two years earlier, in the fall of 1933, Idaho had voted against Prohibition; Shoshone County led the way with a vote of 3,181 to 357.

Still near Silver Cliff Mine above Pottsville (1923).
Part of Stockbridge's work was taking photographs for police evidence. Sheriff R. E. Weniger and Deputy Charlie Bloom are shown here with a still they busted in 1923. Enforcement of the Volstead Act was uncommon in Shoshone County, as evidenced by the conviction in 1929 of Sheriff Weniger and sixty other prominent citizens for wholesale violation of Prohibition laws.

STUDIO PHOTOGRAPHY

✣

OST OF the studio photographs in the Barnard–
Stockbridge collection are attributed to Stockbridge. In
part, this is an accident of history. When the Barnard
Studio was moved to the Barnard Building in 1908, Stockbridge
and Barnard culled the collection and many portraits taken before
that date were discarded, including portraits taken by Barnard
before Stockbridge's arrival. In addition, some early portraits were
lost in the 1890 fire. Stockbridge is also associated with Barnard
Studio portraiture because that was her area of specialty and training.

By 1900, a change was taking place in the type of photographs
that professionals took because of the growing popularity of Kodak
roll-film cameras. There was less novelty involved with photography generally, and consequently less demand for the skills of
itinerant frontier photographers who set up their cameras to record
any interesting scene. Legions of amateurs crowded the field, and
the West was no longer a frontier.

As the frontier was settled, the demand for professional-quality
family album pictures commemorating births, communions, gradu-
ations, weddings, and even deaths remained strong. In fact, the
demand grew as family life was established on the frontier and the

ubiquitous family album was desired for sentimental and social reasons. Such photographs were the mainstay of the Barnard Studio through the years.

Behind her favorite portrait camera, Nellie Stockbridge was animated yet patient. For portrait work she preferred an expensive redwood camera made by Century Camera Company around 1903. It used 5x7 and 8x10 dry-plate glass negatives that she ordered by the box from St. Louis. With cajoling and humoring, Stockbridge would relax her subjects; then with soft light, romantic backdrops, props, and languid poses they would be transformed into something approaching the ideal of the day. The resulting "natural" effect, especially with women and children, was a paradoxical aspect of her studied and exacting perfectionism behind the camera.

It required an acrobatic performance to get the precise lighting, focus, and exposure with children who could not hold a pose, even for a fraction of a second. Stockbridge

(Overleaf) CLOWNS WITH BICYCLES (N.D.)

(Right) ACKERLY BABY WITH TELEPHONE (1911).
A winsome pose, but lacking the Kewpie doll cuteness typical of baby pictures of the time.

BOY IN OVERALLS WITH BALL
(N.D.).
Mothers brought their children by
train or coach from all over the
district to have their pictures
taken by Stockbridge. Usually
children were dressed in their best
Sunday school clothes, to the
dismay of the youngsters. This
photograph of Mrs. D. S. Jones'
son is unusual for its pastoral
quality.

teased, jumped up and down, made ridiculous faces, and resorted to birdlike noises to elicit the desired pose, then leaped behind her camera, checked the focus, and squeezed the bulb to work the shutter—with luck, before the small subject would become alarmed and burst into tears. Though her portrait technique was well within the mainstream of professional portrait photography of her day, her pictures of children were particularly candid and avoided the cloying sentimentality that was the vestige of late-nineteenth-century photography.

Beginning in 1910, the Barnard Studio took official police photographs. In addition to taking pictures of accused criminals for the legal record, starting in 1940, Stockbridge photographed the town's prostitutes as part of their licensing requirement. Stiff, official-looking poses and unretouched photographs portray women in their twenties and thirties, severe in their dress, wearing exaggerated make-up and hairstyles. Afterward, Nellie often posed these same women in relaxed, smiling attitudes that left entirely different impressions. Printed and retouched by Stockbridge or one of her assistants, these informal portraits were bought by the prostitutes as gifts to lovers, friends, and relatives.

Nellie Stockbridge finished her career much as she began it, as a portrait photographer. It is not uncommon to find three generations of Silver Valley residents represented in her files.

AIRPLANE PATENT (N.D.).
Two enterprising gentlemen posed with a model of bird-like wings for a picture to accompany their airplane patent application.

MRS. STANLY A. EASTON AND
CHILDREN (1912).
*In this half-profile of Mrs.
Easton with her children, the
draping of the dress ties the
composition together — a statement
of Stockbridge's studio training.*

YOUNG FIRPO (1925).
*Guido (The Young Bull of
Burke) Bardelli was in the
upswing of his light-heavyweight
boxing career when Stockbridge
took this picture.*

PATRICK MURPHY (1915).
Patrick Murphy was convicted of the murder of "Doc" Cain, the night watchman at the Bunker Hill and Sullivan Mine. Murphy shot Cain through the heart while fleeing from a hold-up at the Depot Bar in Kellogg on August !8, 1915. He pled guilty to first-degree murder and was sentenced to a life term in the Idaho State Penitentiary at Boise. He was pardoned in 1931 at the age of forty-five.

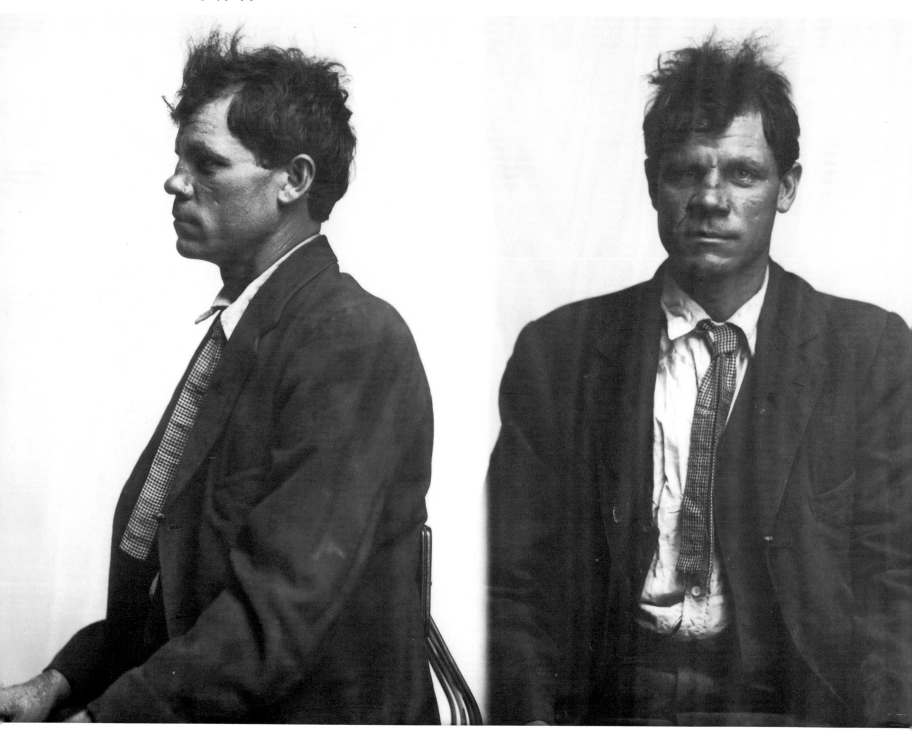

EVELYN ROSS FIELD (1920).
This photograph was one in a series taken of Evelyn Ross Field in which the subject appears in various theatrical costumes, hairstyles, and poses. Here the lady poses barefoot on tiptoe, a la Isadora Duncan. In another picture she is dressed as a high-fashion model, chic from head to toe.

DEWEY SMITH (1912).
Pictures of newspaper and magazine delivery boys were taken for publishers and distributors for promotional and public relations purposes.

LANA TURNER AND MOTHER (N.D.).
Nothing distinguishes this mother-and-daughter portrait from thousands of others taken by Stockbridge, except that the little girl from Burke grew up to be America's sweater girl. Stockbridge presented Lana Turner with a copy of her portrait when Turner passed through Wallace selling war bonds.

THE COLLECTION

Twenty-nine thousand eight hundred thirty-five negatives have been accessioned and cataloged into the Barnard–Stockbridge Collection at the University of Idaho Library. Approximately forty-five hundred are gelatin dry-plate glass negatives; those remaining are flexible film negatives. Eighty-five percent of the total collection consists of portraits; the remaining 15 percent, more than 5,500 negatives, offer a comprehensive overview of the Coeur d'Alene mining region, its industries, and town life.

Through the foresight of two Wallace citizens, Richard Magnuson and Henry Day, the University of Idaho was made aware of the value of these historic negatives before Stockbridge's death. Only weeks after her death and the subsequent donation of the collection to the University of Idaho by Stockbridge's heirs, three University of Idaho librarians drove to Wallace to pick up Stockbridge's working file of several thousand negatives. Made up of 5x7 and 8x10 glass negatives, this file comprised only a small fraction of the negatives known to be stored at the studio.

The working file had been well cared for. The glass negatives were stored in clean envelopes, labeled, and recorded in studio ledgers. They were found to be free from the serious deterioration that results from careless processing, handling, and exposure to excessive dampness or dryness.

It was the library's policy to discard obvious duplicate negatives or those so decomposed or out of focus as to be photographically useless before they became part of the collection. The working file was thus culled, accessioned, and cataloged, incorporating the numbering system Stockbridge had used in her shop ledger. Seventeen hundred study prints were made from this working file, revealing images of remarkable clarity.

Stockbridge had organized the working file into several groups according to what she used them for in the studio. The largest group of negatives, from which she contact printed full-sized prints for sale at the studio, were numbered 1 to 1046 with the prefix X. This category includes Barnard's earliest surviving work in the Coeur d'Alenes and photographs taken since that time considered by Stockbridge to be of aesthetic or historic interest. The X category contains the most comprehensive selection of both mining and town pictures. The majority of the pictures in this book were taken from this category because they represent the range and scope of the photographers' work, record the most interesting historical events, and are, generally, the best preserved and most pleasing.

Another sequence of 168 views is filed under the prefix N. These are photographs of gold-mining activity from the North Fork drainage. Information supplied by the studio ledgers is not infallible and often has been assigned long after the photographs were taken. For example, the ledger that accompanied the Ns was contained in an envelope postmarked 1955. Scratched on the back in Stockbridge's handwriting was the note "List of Views of the North Side taken in 1897." They are all glass 8x10 negatives and, if they were indeed taken in 1897, can confidently be attributed to Barnard.

A third group, prefixed B, consists of 524 views, 96 on 5x7 glass and the balance on flexible film negatives. They are postcard format and were probably used as such in the studio. They represent original work from 1921 to 1954 and copy work from other Barnard Studio negatives. Subjects include important community events, natural disasters, and townscapes.

Group C is a general catch-all category including much copy work on glass and film and negatives that may have been discarded from the X category. This is a small group, numbering only sixty-eight, most of which are on 6½x8½ glass—not a characteristic format for the Barnard Studio. It also includes nine 5x7 and twelve 8x10 glass negatives.

After the University Library had removed the working file of glass negatives from the Barnard Studio in 1965, the studio was taken over by another photographer. When he decided to close the business in 1968, the University Library was again notified and plans were made to retrieve the rest of the Stockbridge and Barnard negatives.

The chore bore little resemblance to the first trip. Boxes of glass and film negatives were stacked from attic to cellar, behind the furnace, and in the rafters, where Stockbridge had presumably put them to get them out of the way. Most of the negatives had been sitting in boxes for thirty years and more. Many of them were stored in old, disintegrating, dusty envelopes and were brittle. It was known that most of the negatives were portraits. Fortunately, 95 percent of the portraits were identified in studio ledgers. The unofficial but conservative estimate of the total number of negatives brought to the library from the studio was 100,000.

Ordinarily, portrait collections would not be copied from disintegrating negatives, cataloged, or printed because of the tremendous expense involved. However, because so many of the portrait negatives were identified, and because the Coeur d'Alenes were settled by people of many ethnic origins, the portraits were deemed to be of considerable social and historical value. For the time being, however, the portrait negatives were stored and priorities were set concerning the cataloging of the non-portrait negatives first.

Besides the portrait material tied to studio ledgers of which 24,588 negatives were finally cataloged, three other distinct groups of negatives were identified. The largest group, with the prefix P, contains 1,636 portraits on 5x7 glass negatives that were taken before the studio ledger was started. Another group, the Os, numbers 1,216, of which about half are portraits and group portraits on 8x10 glass negatives. There are four 11x14 glass negatives in this group that were taken between 1899 and 1905. The rest

---

(Overleaf) IDAHO MINE (N.D.).
Though the man overlooking the Idaho Mine is unidentified in the ledger, he bears striking resemblance to the photographer T. N. Barnard.

are 8x10 glass of miscellaneous subjects. A final group of 589 negatives, given the prefix A, includes another six 11x14 glass negatives, the rest measuring 8x10. The photographs include a series taken for the Mine Owners Association, a picture of Barnard's son's corpse (which establishes that the earliest material dates back at least to 1893), and miscellaneous mining views.

A very complex problem faced the University of Idaho Library in 1977. A significant portion of the remaining uncataloged negatives were on nitrocellulose-based film, which, under certain conditions, can ignite. It was pointed out that under the worst possible combination of circumstances, the nitrocellulose negatives stored in the library's basement could explode, causing extensive damage. This information was not casually received. A fund-raising drive, headed by Henry Day, was put in motion to pay for the copying of the nitrocellulose film onto 35mm safety film. Simultaneously, all the remaining uncataloged negatives were culled and cataloging was begun. Seven thousand nitrocellulose negatives were salvaged and successfully copied onto safety film by October, 1979. Cataloging the entire collection, reduced to 29,835 images, was completed in April, 1982. The cataloging of the collection and the printing of selected negatives were supported by grants from the Association for the Humanities in Idaho and the National Endowment for the Humanities respectively. Archival prints of Barnard–Stockbridge photographs are sold by the University of Idaho Library Special Collections, who will supply a price guide upon request (University of Idaho Library Special Collections, Moscow, Idaho 83843).

To date, no Barnard or Stockbridge negatives outside the collection have come to light, though many original prints from negatives not in the Barnard–Stockbridge Collection exist in photographic archives scattered throughout Idaho and Washington, and in private collections.

One particularly relevant collection of prints is the Barnard–Huffman collection housed at the Museum of Native American Cultures in Spokane, Washington. The collection consists of 118 mounted prints donated to MONAC by Enoch and William Barnard, sons of T. N.

Barnard. Fifteen of the prints are Barnard photographs and are single images mounted on matboard, in formats ranging from $4\frac{1}{2}$ x $7\frac{3}{8}$ inches to $7\frac{1}{2}$ x $4\frac{1}{2}$ inches. Three of the Barnard photographs were taken in the Coeur d'Alenes; twelve were taken in Montana and are of Crow Indians and the United States cavalry. With the exception of three Yellowstone views taken by F. Jay Haynes, the balance of the pictures were taken by L. A. Huffman and are representative of Huffman's work in Montana. Because most of the pictures were taken in the early 1880s when Barnard and Huffman were associates in Montana, and because those taken by Barnard give us the clearest idea of Huffman's influence on Barnard, the collection is of particular interest.

Barnard was directly influenced by Huffman, for whom he worked, and indirectly influenced by Haynes through Huffman's association with Haynes. Fortunately, both of their working collections have survived and are presently housed at the Montana Historical Society in Helena.

The F. Jay Haynes Collection consists of 9,000 glass negatives and is completely cataloged by a modified Library of Congress cataloging system. An index of the collection is available on microfiche.

The Huffman Collection has been given by Huffman's family to the Montana Historical Society, which has agreed to catalog it and restore any negatives that might require it. The collection was in commercial use until recently. There are 1,500 items in the collection, both glass negatives and 5x7 flexible film negatives.

The Haynes, Huffman, and Barnard–Stockbridge collections together provide an excellent overview of frontier photography in Montana and Idaho. In addition, the three collections can be seen as a continuum, as the art and profession of photography were handed down from teacher to apprentice.

SELECT BIBLIOGRAPHY

PHOTOGRAPHY

There are several excellent, readable histories of photography. We have primarily used two as references: Robert Taft's *Photography and the American Scene: A Social History 1839–1889* (reprint edition; New York: Dover Publications, 1964 [1938]) and Halmut Gernsheim's comprehensive *History of Photography: From Camera Obscura to the Beginning of the Modern Era* (New York: McGraw-Hill Book Co., 1969). Taft gives thorough treatment to the development and adoption by Americans of various photographic forms and devotes several chapters to their uses in the West. Gernsheim's book is encyclopedic in scope and arranged for easy use.

Not a history, but extremely helpful to anyone making use of a photographic collection, is Robert A. Weinstein and Larry Booth, *Collection, Use, and Care of Historical Photographs* (Nashville: American Association for State and Local History, 1977). It is perfectly understandable to the layperson and an essential resource for anyone responsible for photographic materials.

Three books attempt to discuss some aspect of photography in the West. *Era of Exploration: The Rise of Landscape Photography in the American West, 1860–1885,* by Weston J. Naef in collaboration with James N. Wood (New York: Albright–Knox Art Gallery and the Metropolitan Museum of Art, 1975), is both a beautifully printed catalog of landscape photographs and a succinct history of American landscape photography. An essay is followed by a chronology and chapters on five photographers. Dorothy and Thomas Hoobler have written a concise overview of frontier photography in *Photographing the Frontier* (New York: G. P. Putnam's Sons, 1980), which emphasizes the text and uses the photographs only as illustration. *Photographers of the Frontier West,* by Ralph W. Andrews (Seattle: Superior Publishing Co., 1965), suffers from being neither comprehensive nor particularly selective in the choice of eleven frontier photographers discussed. It is badly designed and the photographs are poorly reproduced.

The careers of F. Jay Haynes and Laton A. Huffman are directly related to those of Barnard and Stockbridge. Of the three books on Haynes, *Following the Frontier with F. Jay Haynes,* by Freeman Tilden (New York: Alfred A. Knopf, 1964), is a very readable biography but is not chronologically organized, making it difficult to use for reference. The other two books are primarily collections of Haynes' photographs: *F. Jay Haynes, Photographer* (Helena: Montana Historical Society, 1981) and *Northern Pacific Views: The Railroad Photography of F. Jay Haynes, 1876–1905* (Helena: Montana Historical Society Press, 1983).

There are two books about Laton A. Huffman, essentially the same in format and approach. Both are photographic books accompanied by text that draws heavily on Huffman's letters and other personal papers. *Before Barbed Wire,* by Mark H. Brown and William R. Felton (New York: Henry Holt & Co., 1956), includes Huffman photographs of ranch life and cowboys, while *The Frontier Years: L. A. Huffman, Photographer of the Plains,* by the same authors (New York: Henry Holt & Co., 1955), is an overview of the photographer's career.

IDAHO

The basic multi-volume histories of Idaho are useful because they reflect the times in which they were written and because they all carry biographical sketches of personalities considered important at those times. *History of Idaho,* by Hiram Taylor French (Chicago: Lewis Publishing Co., 1914); *History of Idaho,* edited by James H. Hawley (Chicago: S. J. Clarke, 1920); and *Idaho: The Place and its People: A History of the Gem State from Prehistory to Present Days,* by Byron Defenbach (Chicago: American Historical Society, 1933), are all basically political histories with sections boosting the economic advantages of the state. The history edited by Hawley has the advantage of his personal knowledge of the Coeur d'Alene district. The best of the multivolume histories of Idaho, especially in its coverage of the Coeur d'Alenes, is Merrill D. Beal and Merle W. Wells, *History of Idaho* (New York: Lewis Historical Publishing Co., 1959). Wells has done other work on North Idaho that provides a solid basis for the sections on the Coeur d'Alenes.

All four of these histories include at least one volume of short biographies of important Idaho persons. While the selections by no means stand the test of history (and were in many cases written by the subjects), they do provide a starting place for tracing careers and family influence.

A basic reference tool for using library sources pertaining to Idaho is *Idaho Local History: A Bibliography with Checklist of Library Holdings,* by Milo G. Nelson and Charles A. Webbert (Moscow: University Press of Idaho, 1976). It is a comprehensive holdings list for Idaho's state and university libraries at the date of publication.

THE REGION

The most useful chronicle of early northern Idaho history is *An Illustrated History of North Idaho* ([Spokane?]: Western Historical Publishing Co., 1903), a publishing effort intended to promote the region and be purchased by its citizens. It is a surprisingly useful, fact-filled, and directly written account of towns and counties in the area, the more so because it was published during the lifetimes of most of the participants in the events it recounts. Richard G. Magnuson performed a service for all historians of the Coeur d'Alenes when he wrote up the history of the area from 1884 to 1894 in the form of a chronology of events mentioned in the daily newspapers of the time in *Coeur d'Alene Diary: The First Ten Years of Hardrock Mining in North Idaho* (Portland, Oregon: Metropolitan Press, 1968). Magnuson is an unofficial historian of the Coeur d'Alenes and

has a large collection of original documents and other artifacts from the early days.

In 1937, on the occasion of the fiftieth anniversary of the city of Wallace, both of the local newspapers published special supplements on the history of the town and the region, which are useful in providing information about specific businesses and personalities: "Fifty Years of Progress; historical-progressive edition of the Coeur d'Alenes" (Wallace, Idaho: Special edition of the *Wallace Miner,* December 16, 1937), and "The Golden Anniversary Edition, *1887-1937*" (Wallace: *Coeur d'Alene Press,* 1937).

Finally, there are a number of more or less personal accounts of the Coeur d'Alene area. They tell the story, rather than the history, of the mining district and have to be checked against more factual material. Although biased, they can be quite readable. Among them are William T. Stoll, *Silver Strike: The True Story of Silver Mining in the Coeur d'Alenes, As Told To W. H. Whicker* (Boston: Little, Brown & Co., 1932); Flora Cloman (Mrs. Victor Clement), *I'd Live it Over* (New York: Farrar and Rinehart, 1941); and Russell Arden Bankson and Lester S. Harrison, *Beneath these Mountains* (New York: Vantage Press, 1967). More a collection of stories than a personal memoir is *Gems of Thought and History of Shoshone County,* edited by George C. Hobson and sponsored by the Allied Fraternities Council, Shoshone County (Kellogg: Kellogg Evening Press, 1940).

While we used sources of national scope for background on various activities and occupations, sources dealing specifically with Idaho and with the region were of more direct use. The timber industry in northern Idaho is discussed by Clarence C. Strong and Clyde W. Webb in *White Pine: King of Many Waters* (Missoula, Montana: Mountain Press, 1970). The Northern Pacific Railroad, the Union Pacific, and more local lines are discussed by John Fahey in *Inland Empire: D. C. Corbin and Spokane* (Seattle: University of Washington Press, 1965); by John V. Wood in *Railroads through the Coeur d'Alenes* (Caldwell, Idaho: Caxton Printers, 1983); and by Harry Edward Bilger in "History of Railroads in Idaho" (master's thesis, University of Idaho, 1969). Prohibition was not a great success in northern Idaho; Edison Klein Putman tells the story for the whole state in "The Prohibition Movement in Idaho, 1863–1934" (Ph.D. dissertation, University of Idaho, 1979).

Although they were members of the same political party, United States Senator Weldon Heyburn of Wallace and President Theodore Roosevelt clashed over many issues—the most important being the establishment of national forests in the West. Rufus Cook discusses Heyburn in "A Study of the Career of Weldon Brinton Heyburn through his First Term in the United States Senate, 1852–1909" (master's thesis, University of Idaho, 1964), and Joseph Bucklin Bishop includes some relevant letters in *Theodore Roosevelt and his Time Shown in his Own Letters* (New York: Charles Scribner's Sons, 1920).

The story of Catholic Church activity in the Coeur d'Alenes has not been recorded in a single volume; much of the early Wallace record, often written in French, has been lost. However, the *Chronicle of Catholic History of the Pacific Northwest, 1743–1960,* by Wilfred S. Schoenberg, S.J. (Spokane, Washington: Gonzaga Preparatory School, 1962), gives a coherent outline of church activity.

The more social side of the Coeur d'Alenes is touched on in Charles E. Lauterbach's *Pioneer Theatre in the West: Life and Times of John S. Langrishe* (Boise, Idaho: Boise State University Center for Research, Grants, and Contracts, 1979).

Captain John Mullan described what he found during his historic work on the road that then bore his name in *Miners and Travelers' Guide to Oregon, Washington, Idaho, Montana, Wyoming, and Colorado, via the Missouri and Columbia Rivers* (reprint edition; New York: Arno Press, 1973 [1865]). Ruby El Hult has written a popular account of the boats on Lake Coeur d'Alene, *Steamboats in the Timber* (Caldwell, Idaho: Caxton Printers, 1952, 1968).

The most devastating natural disaster known in Idaho's history was the holocaust that swept through the forests of northern Idaho in 1910, burning half of Wallace. In addition to Forest Service documentation of the event, there are three books that tell the story in popular fashion: Betty G. Spencer, *The Big Blowup* (Caldwell, Idaho: Caxton Printers, 1956); Ruby El Hult, *Northwest Disaster: Avalanche and Fire*

(Portland, Oregon: Binfords & Mort, 1960); and Stan Cohen, *The Big Burn: The Northwest's Forest Fire of 1910* (Missoula, Montana: Pictorial Histories Publishing Co., 1978).

COMMUNITY

Of the many works on small towns in American life, Richard Lingeman's *Small Town America: A Narrative History, 1620–The Present* (New York: G. P. Putnam's Sons, 1980) is the most recent and is very comprehensive. *Main Street on the Middle Border,* by Lewis Atherton (Bloomington: Indiana University Press, 1954), is useful in describing business life in a small town.

Polk business directories for the Coeur d'Alene towns and local telephone books provide confirmation of business locations and ownership. Used together with Sanborn insurance maps for Wallace, Murray, Wardner, and Burke (New York: Sanborn Map Co., various dates), the directories give a graphic and concrete picture of these communities.

MINING—GENERAL

Walter Crane's *Gold and Silver* (New York: John Wiley & Sons, 1908) is an economic history of mining in the United States that correlates geographical, historical, geological, and technical statistics and information.

Placer formation, simple mining methods, and application of those methods in Idaho are covered in W. W. Staley, *Elementary Methods of Placer Mining* (Pamphlet 35; Moscow: Idaho Bureau of Mines and Geology, 1931). Particularly helpful for understanding large-scale gold-mining techniques is *Gold Mining Machinery, Its Selection, Arrangement, & Installation,* by W. H. Tinney (New York: D. Van Nostrand Co., 1906), a handbook for mine managers and engineers describing methods and machinery used at the time.

The best introduction to turn-of-the-century mining techniques is Robert Peele's first edition of the *Mining Engineers' Handbook* (New York: John Wiley & Sons, 1918).

It became the bible of the profession in its time and is understandable and well organized. More difficult to use, but still of interest, is the *Handbook of Mining Details* prepared by the staff of the *Engineering and Mining Journal* (New York: McGraw-Hill Book Co., 1912).

Of more specific use are W. L. Saunders, "History of the Rock Drill," *Mining and Scientific Press* 100 (May 21, 1910): 735, and Charles H. Foreman, "Mining Methods of the Coeur d'Alene Mining District," *Mining Congress Journal* 21 (May 1935): 84–85. A pamphlet entitled "Mining Salutes Idaho's Fifty Years of Statehood 1890–1940" (Boise: Idaho Mining Association, 1940) provides information on mining methods and an indication of how the mine owners viewed the miner's life.

GOLD-MINING ERA

There is no comprehensive history of gold mining in the Coeur d'Alenes, nor is the gold rush of 1883–1884 given more than cursory treatment in general histories of mining in the West. An unpublished study, Robert Wayne Smith's "History of Placer and Quartz Gold Mining in the Coeur d'Alenes" (master's thesis, University of Idaho, 1932), is the most reliable and readable work on the subject. The author made use of interviews with pioneers and some original source material not available to the public. An account by travel writer Eugene Smalley published in the October, 1884, issue of *Century Magazine* (and reprinted in *Idaho Yesterdays* 11 [Fall 1967]: 2–10) entitled "The Coeur d'Alene Stampede" gives a first-hand acount of life in the goldfields. Further impressions of boom-town society can be gathered through scattered issues of early North Side newspapers available on microfilm: *Coeur d'Alene Nugget* (Eagle City), *Coeur d'Alene Sun* (Murray), and *Idaho Sun* (Murray).

Two promotional publications issued by the Northern Pacific Railroad deserve credit for creating the gold rush to the Coeur d'Alenes. "The Gold Fields of the Coeur d'Alenes," written by Newton H. Chittenden (Circular 12, The World's Guide for Home, Health, Gold, and Pleasure Seekers Series; St. Paul, Minnesota, 1884), prepared travelers for the trip to the goldfields. "In the Gold Fields of Coeur d'Alenes" (Chicago: Rand McNally, n.d.) told the prospectors what to expect when they got there.

Two publications of the Idaho Bureau of Mines and Geology discuss gold mining on the North Fork of the Coeur d'Alene River. *Gold in Idaho,* by W. W. Staley (Pamphlet 68; second edition, Moscow: Idaho Bureau of Mines and Geology, 1960), includes production figures and a map of claims. More specific is *Gold-Bearing Gravels near Murray, Idaho,* by Wakefield Dort, Jr. (Pamphlet 116; Moscow: Idaho Bureau of Mines and Geology, 1958), which discusses land formation and mining methods employed on the North Side. The impact of mining technology on the Coeur d'Alene River valley is described in *River of Green and Gold,* by Fred W. Rabe and David C. Flaherty (Natural Resources Series 4; Moscow: Idaho Research Foundation, 1974). One chapter is devoted to the impact of gold mining on the North Fork of the Coeur d'Alene River.

SILVER MINING

Two well-documented books were published in 1979 dealing with hard-rock mining in the West. Both Ronald C. Brown's *Hard-Rock Miners: The Intermountain West, 1860–1920* (College Station: Texas A&M University Press, 1979) and Mark Wyman's *Hard Rock Epic: Western Miners and the Industrial Revolution, 1860–1910* (Berkeley: University of California Press, 1979) have presented, essentially for the first time, the history of western underground mining through an analysis of the lives of the miners themselves. By focusing on social history, Brown and Wyman have added to the previous studies done of politicians, unions, and mining magnates. Unfortunately for the student of Idaho or Montana mining history, Brown did not cover these two states. Wyman is more analytical, examining what he calls the "dual frontiers of the American West and Industrial Revolution." He does cover Idaho and the Coeur d'Alene mining district.

Good background material on early underground mining can be found in Otis Young's *Black Powder and Hand Steel: Mines and Machines on the Old Western Frontier* (Norman: University of Oklahoma Press, 1976), although he restricts his coverage to mining before 1880 and to the southern Rockies.

Two local mine owners have provided information from personal knowledge on the history of silver mining in the Coeur d'Alenes: Henry Day in "Mining Highlights of the Coeur d'Alene District," *Idaho Yesterdays* 7 (Winter 1963–64): 2–9; and W. Earl Greenough in *First Hundred Years of the Coeur d'Alene Mining Region* (Mullan, Idaho, 1947). Another early reminiscence is E. Thomas, "Early Days in the Coeur d'Alene Mining District," *Mining Congress Journal* 10 (September 1924): 404–407. *An Economic History of North Idaho, 1800–1900,* by D. E. Livingston-Little (Los Angeles: L. L. and C. S. Morrison, 1965), does a solid job on the Coeur d'Alene district in the early days.

Among the technical reports done on the Coeur d'Alenes in the early years, none can compare to Frederick L. Ransome and Frank Cathcart Calkins, *The Geology and Ore Deposits of the Coeur d'Alene District, Idaho,* Professional Paper 62, United States Geological Survey, Department of the Interior (Washington, D.C.: Government Printing Office, 1908). It is a large book, written primarily for the geologist, but its sections on history and mining methods are understandable by and useful to the layperson. In contrast, the annual reports of Idaho's Inspector of Mines in the first decade of this century are mostly promotional pieces for mines owned by friends of the Inspector.

Among useful first-hand and personal accounts are Henry L. Day's "Mining and Milling Practice of Forty Years Ago in the Coeur d'Alenes" (speech given December 2, 1966, to the Northwest Mining Association; the Day Northwest Collection, University of Idaho Library) and Frank A. Crampton's *Deep Enough* (Denver: Sage Books, 1956).

The major book on the Hercules Mine is John Fahey's *The Days of the Hercules* (Moscow: University Press of Idaho, 1978). James Montgomery provides a popular account of Hercules owner May Arkwright Hutton in his *Liberated Woman* (Spokane, Washington: Gingko House, 1974).

More nonsense has been written about the discovery of the Bunker Hill and Sullivan mines than about any other event in the history of the Coeur d'Alenes; it is rivaled only by the myths surrounding the blowing up of the mill in 1899. D. E. Livingston-Little, in "The Bunker Hill and Sullivan: North Idaho's Mining Development from 1885 to 1900," *Idaho Yesterdays* 16 (Spring 1963): 34–43, and T. A. Rickard's chapter on the Bunker Hill enterprise in his *History of American Mining* (New York: McGraw-Hill Book Co., 1932) tell the early story of the company as straightforwardly as anyone has.

The various twists and turns of the history of the Morning Mine have been told by John Fahey in *Ballyhoo Bonanza: Charles Sweeny and the Idaho Mines* (Seattle: University of Washington Press, 1971) and by Isaac F. Marcosson in *Metal Magic: The Story of the American Smelting and Refining Company* (New York: Farrar, Straus, 1949).

The story of the Hecla Mine had to be pieced together from newspapers and other sources, with the help of a twelve-page mimeographed "History of the Hecla Mining Company," by Robert E. Sorenson (Wallace, Idaho: Hecla Mining Co., 1962).

The power elites of western mining have been examined by Richard H. Peterson in *The Bonanza Kings: The Social Origins and Business Behavior of Western Mining Entrepreneurs, 1870–1900* (Lincoln: University of Nebraska Press, 1971) and by Clark C. Spence in *Mining Engineers and the American West: The Lace-Boot Brigade, 1849–1933* (New Haven, Connecticut: Yale University Press, 1970). Peterson includes only one Coeur d'Alene mine owner, Simeon Reed of the Bunker Hill; Spence talks about several of the famous Idaho mining engineers—John Hays Hammond, Victor M. Clement, and Frederick W. Bradley.

MINING WARS

The basic survey of the union movement in the West leading up to the first mining war in the Coeur d'Alenes in 1892 is Richard E. Lingenfelter's *Hardrock Miners: A History of the Mining Labor Movement in the American West 1863–1893* (Berkeley: University of California Press, 1974). He does a good job of describing the Coeur d'Alene encounter in one of his last chapters, relying for much of his information on the basic secondary source: *The Coeur d'Alene Mining War of*

1892, by Robert Wayne Smith (reprint edition, Cambridge, Massachusetts: Peter Smith, 1968 [1961]). Smith's classic remains basically unchanged from his doctoral dissertation on the subject, done at the University of California in the 1930s after he had taught for several years in Wallace. Smith did an excellent job of separating myth from reality at a time when some of the participants in the mining wars were still alive.

Unfortunately, no one has yet done similarly thorough work on the 1899 war. Vernon Jensen has included a good description of events in his *Heritage of Conflict: Labor Relations in the Nonferrous Metals Industry up to 1930* (Ithaca, New York: Cornell University Press, 1968 [1950]), which covers the entire story of the Western Federation of Miners in some depth. Stewart Holbrook wrote a popular account of the various mining conflicts in the Rocky Mountains, including the Coeur d'Alenes, entitled *The Rocky Mountain Revolution* (New York: Henry Holt & Co., 1956), which is very readable but suffers from a highly dramatic view of the miners and their unions.

Charles Siringo was an active participant in the events of 1892, possibly even a cause of some of them, as a Pinkerton detective working as an undercover spy in the union camp. He wrote vivid, dime-novel-type accounts of his undeniably exciting exploits that place him at the center of the action and justify his position: "The Trouble in the Coeur d'Alene, A Chapter from Wild World Magazine, V. 63, no. 1" (London: A. Newnes, n.d.) and *Two Evil Isms* (Chicago: C. Siringo, 1915). Siringo's bias is more than balanced by May Arkwright Hutton in *The Coeur d'Alenes or a Tale of the Modern Inquisition in Idaho* (Denver: App Engraving and Printing Co., 1900), in which the mine owners can do no right.

The conflict in interpretation of what happened in 1899 in the Coeur d'Alenes started immediately after the physical confrontation stopped. This colored the official United States government investigations into the clash, which were demanded by union supporters but were controlled by congressional friends of big business. Nevertheless, these reports are basic documents providing eyewitness testimony, official correspondence, and accurate information on dates and troop movements, in the context of justifying federal military support of the mine owners' position. The three major reports are *Coeur d'Alene Mining Troubles, Letter from the Secretary of War* (U.S. Congress, Senate, 56th Cong., 1st sess., 1900, S. Doc. 142); *Labor Troubles in Idaho* (U.S. Congress, Senate, 56th Cong., 1st sess., 1899, S. Doc. 42); and *Coeur d'Alene Labor Troubles* (U.S. Congress, House, Committee on Military Affairs, 56th Cong., 1st sess., 1900, H. Rept. 1999).

The effects of the 1899 conflict on labor relations in the Coeur d'Alenes are examined by Stanley Stewart Phipps in "From Bull Pen to Bargaining Table: The Tumultuous Struggle of the Coeur d'Alene Miners for the Right to Organize, 1887–1942" (Ph.D. dissertation, University of Idaho, 1983) and on national affairs by David H. Grover in *Debaters and Dynamiters: The Story of the Haywood Trial* (Corvallis: Oregon State University Press, 1964). Phipps sympathizes with the workers he writes about, while Grover appears convinced that Orchard told the truth and Haywood was guilty of the conspiracy of which he was acquitted.

The crucial matter of martial law and its place in a democratic society is dealt with by Charles Fairman in *Law of Martial Rule* (Chicago: Callaghan & Co., 1930). Regrettably, no one has done any work on the complex question of the use of black federal troops to put down labor movements.

One stumbling block to doing basic research on the 1899 mining wars is the lack of local newspapers from 1898 and 1899 in university and regional libraries. The closest newspaper available for research with editions from those years is the *Spokesman-Review,* formerly the *Spokane Review.*

NEWSPAPERS

Many early Idaho newspapers have been microfilmed, but only an incomplete index to the early territorial newspapers is available. The most current and comprehensive list of Idaho newspapers is *University of Idaho Newspaper Holdings as of December 31, 1979,* compiled by Charles Webbert (Moscow: University of Idaho Library, 1979).

Both major and minor events of the Coeur d'Alenes were recorded in the Spokane *Spokesman-Review* (title varies), indexed for the years 1887–1920. The index is arranged alphabetically, both by town or region and by subject. This makes the index particularly useful in pin-pointing a date when the subject or event is known, and in turn aids in the use of the unindexed Idaho newspapers.

We have used the following Idaho newspaper sources in our research for this book: *Idaho Daily Statesman* (Boise); *Silver Star* (Burke); *Coeur d'Alene Press* (Coeur d'Alene); *Coeur d'Alene Nugget* (Eagle City); *Kellogg Evening News; Mullan Mirror; Mullan Daily News; Coeur d'Alene Sun* and *Idaho Sun* (Murray); *Coeur d'Alene American, Coeur d'Alene Miner, Idaho Press, Wallace Free Press, Wallace Miner, Wallace Press, Wallace Press-Times, North Idaho Press, Daily Press Times,* and *The Daily Times* (Wallace); and *Coeur d'Alene Barbarian* and *Wardner News* (Wardner).

Other newspaper sources include the *Spokesman–Review* and *Northwest Mining Truth* (Spokane) and the *New York Times.*

T. N. BARNARD AND NELLIE STOCKBRIDGE

The history of Thomas Nathan Barnard has been recreated in a biographical mosaic composed of small pieces of information from many sources. There is a short, half-column biography in *An Illustrated History of North Idaho* (1903, see listing under THE REGION), which was probably written by Barnard himself. Very helpful were two collections of personal papers, newspaper clippings, letters, and other documents held by his descendants: his great-granddaughter Cirrelda Mills of Boulder, Colorado, and his daughter-in-law, Mrs. William Barnard, of Spokane, Washington. The latter group has been donated to the University of Idaho Library to be included with the Barnard–Stockbridge collection.

Barnard's Iowa origins are found in the biography of his father, Charles Barnard, in the *History of Winneshiek and Allamakee Counties* by W. E. Alexander (Sioux City, Iowa: Western Publishing Company, 1882). The relationship between T. N. Barnard and Laton Huffman was traced through cemetery records, censuses, obituaries, and documents from both families.

The main sources for information about Barnard's life in Wallace, in addition to family papers, are news items and studio advertisements in the various Wallace papers and the *Spokesman–Review* from 1885 to 1907. Barnard's only photographic publication, *Coeur d'Alene Towns, Mines, Mountains, and Lakes,* was published and copyrighted in 1891 by him in Wallace and was printed by Druck v. Louis Glaser, Leipzig and New York. A short history of the studio is contained in *Fifty Years of Progress,* published by the *Wallace Miner* on December 16, 1937. Barnard's investments in both mines and real estate are listed in the more than sixty transactions recorded under his name at the Shoshone County Courthouse in Wallace from 1887 to his will in 1915.

Most newspaper accounts of Nellie Stockbridge's life date from the late 1950s and 1960s, when the photographer was in her eighties and nineties. Of these, the two most reliable stories appear in the June 10, 1958, issue of the *North Idaho Press* and the June 9, 1957, issue of the *Spokesman–Review Magazine.* A fanciful version of the studio history was published in the September 11, 1966, issue of the *Spokesman–Review,* of which the authors have a copy annotated by Enoch Barnard (son of T. N. Barnard). A similar account was published in the *Salt Lake Tribune Home Magazine* with additional misinformation and fictitious detail.

Ruth Ray of Oklahoma City, Stockbridge's niece by her sister Elva Ray, provided excerpts of her aunt's correspondence, a copy of a family history written by Nellie Stockbridge, much background information concerning Stockbridge's upbringing, and personal reminiscences about the family. Two of Nellie Stockbridge's sisters lived in Wallace at the time of her arrival there: Grace, the district's first woman bookkeeper, and Clara, who was married to the Rev. Henry S. Black, a Baptist minister. All five of the Stockbridge children lived in the Northwest at one time, making the family history particularly valuable. Most of the information was provided in an interview at Ruth Ray's home in November, 1979. Further information was provided in correspondence with Ray, with Mrs. Helen E. Henrickson, Stockbridge's niece by her sister Grace, and with Fred Stockbridge, Stockbridge's nephew by her brother Fred.

Documents provided some useful dates and interesting facts: business transactions between Barnard and Stockbridge concerning the studio are recorded in deeds; Stockbridge's will and testament, dated April 24, 1963, produced the name of a close personal friend, Ida Mortimor, whose daughter, Mrs. Eleanor Mortimor Diltz, knew the photographer in the rare, nonprofessional role of family friend.

The Polk directory of 1905 revealed Stockbridge lived with the T. N. Barnard family at that time. A reference in the Mining Inspector's Report of 1914 listed Stockbridge and T. N. Barnard as associates in the Cassidy Gold Mining Co., demonstrating Stockbridge was not immune to speculation—indeed, she left some penny stocks to her heirs.

Generations of many Coeur d'Alene families had their pictures taken by Stockbridge, and interviews with those who can recall her tend to reinforce the image of her as a spry, very professional businesswoman of formidable age.

Copies of materials used by the authors, including notes from interviews, have been donated to the University of Idaho Library.

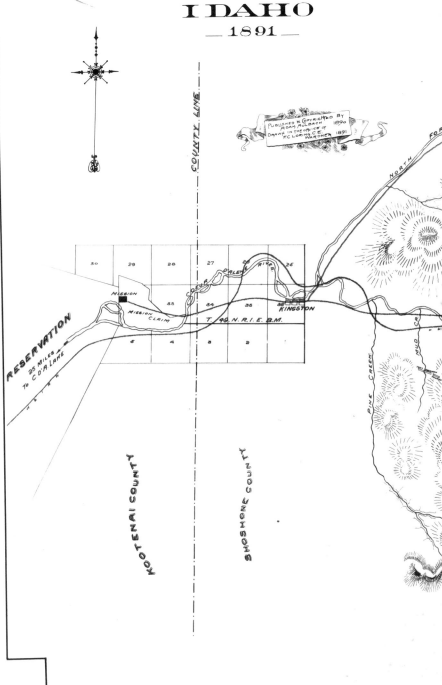

MAP OF THE COEUR D'ALENE MINING REGION COMMISSIONED BY ADAM AULBACH (N.D.).

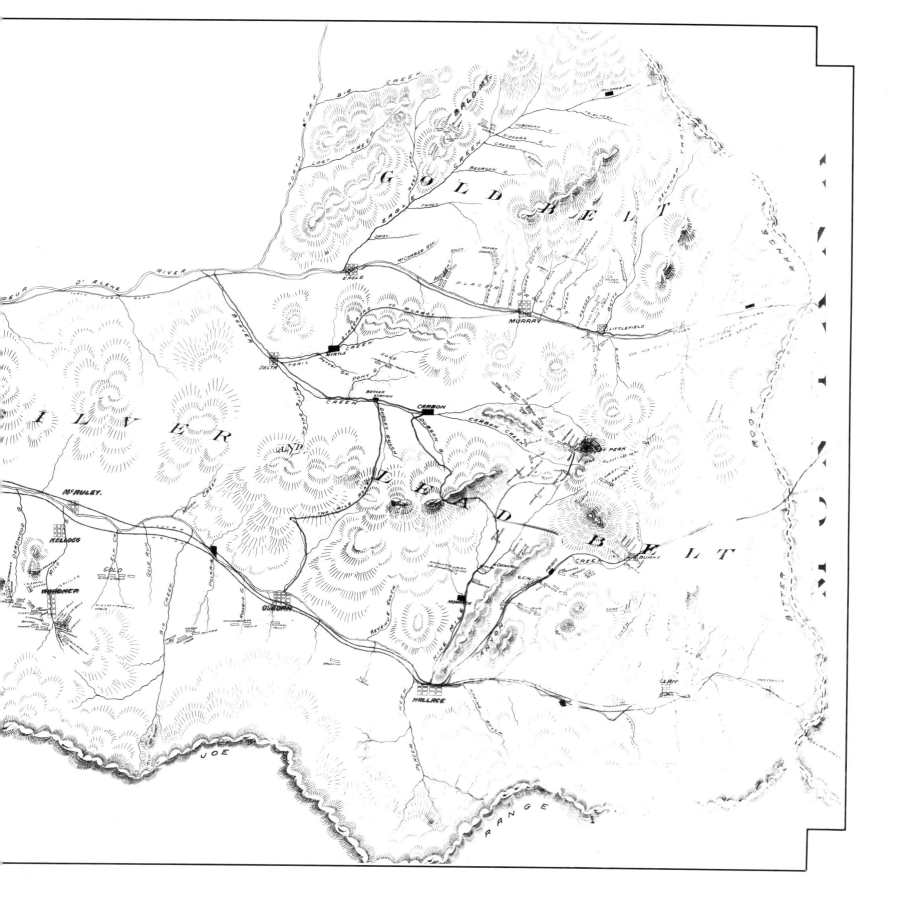

LIST OF PLATES

x BARNARD WITH CIGAR (8-A35a)

3 THOMAS NATHAN BARNARD IN MONTANA (Wm. Barnard papers)

4 BARNARD FAMILY, FRIENDS, AND HOUSE, WALLACE (8-X51a)

7 NELLIE STOCKBRIDGE AS A YOUNG WOMAN (Portrait collection)

9 PORTRAIT CAMERA (Authors' papers)

11 EARLY PICTURE OF THE BARNARD STUDIO GIFT SHOP (Authors' papers)

12 NELLIE STOCKBRIDGE IN HER NINETIES (Portrait collection)

14 MOTHER LODE BOYS (8-X993)

16 SNYBAR CABIN (8-N96)

17 MURRAY, 1890 (8-B224)

18 ARCHIE SMITH IN FRONT OF HIS CABIN (8-X552)

21 MOTHER LODE MILL AT LITTLEFIELD (8-X515)

22 ARIZONA PLACER MINE, HYDRAULICKING IN DREAM GULCH (8-X8)

23 ARIZONA PLACER MINE SHOWING SLUICES AND RIFFLES (8-X11)

24 PLACER MINING, DELTA (8-X302)

26 TIN CUP GROUP, HERCULES MINE (8-X433)

28 SINGLE-JACKING CONTEST, MULLAN (8-B216-58)

29 SINGLE-JACKING CONTEST, MULLAN, *left* (8-B216-60) and *right* (8-B216-65)

30 MORNING MINE, INTERIOR SHOWING CAGES (8-X400)

31 BUTTE AND COEUR D'ALENE MINE, MEN DRILLING, (8-X903e)

33 SUCCESS MINE INTERIOR (8-X366c)

36 HERCULES MINE AND MILL (8-X147c)

37 GROUSE GULCH COMPRESSOR, MORNING MINE (8-X1030a)

39 ORIGINAL "GLORY HOLE" AT BUNKER HILL AND SULLIVAN MINE (8-X24)

41 HECLA MINE EXTERIOR (8-X152)

42 HERCULES MINE OWNERS, SHORTLY AFTER DISCOVERING SILVER (8-X547)

45 LEAD SILVER MINING COMPANY KITCHEN (8-A159-1)

46 SNOWSTORM BOARDINGHOUSE (8-X251)

48 FRISCO MINE AND MILL (8-X134)

50 FRISCO MILL BEFORE 1892 EXPLOSION (8-X1023a)

51 FRISCO MILL AFTER 1892 EXPLOSION (8-X85)

52 TWENTY-SECOND U.S. INFANTRY AT WALLACE, 1892 (8-X483)

55 FEDERAL TROOP ENCAMPMENT, WALLACE, 1892 (8-X473)

59 BUNKER HILL AND SULLIVAN MILL, AFTER EXPLOSION, 1899 (8-X14a)

60 BUNKER HILL AND SULLIVAN MILL, AFTER EXPLOSION, 1899 (8-X13a)

61 MILITARY OFFICERS (8-0500-J) uncataloged

63 GENERAL VIEW OF THE BULLPEN, KELLOGG, 1899 (8-X29a)

65 INTERIOR OF THE BULL PEN, SHOWING BUNKS (8-X536)

67 MEN DRILLING WITH WOODEN GUNS (8-X312)

68 DISPLAY OF IWW LITERATURE (8-0580)

69 MEN EATING IN THE BULL PEN (8-X27)

70 WALLACE, 1889 (8-X1048a)

73 BURKE, 1888 (8-X431)

74 BURKE, 1912 (8-X37)

76 WARDNER, 1907 (8-X282)

77 WARDNER, TAKEN FROM THE LAST CHANCE MINE (8-X283)

78 *COLFAX* (8-B519)

80 *GEORGIE OAKES* (8-B427)

81 MCRAE'S STAGE (8-X186)

82 ENGINEER P. SHEELEY STANDING BY U.P. ENGINE NO. 3513 (8-X878a)

83 OREGON RAILWAY AND NAVIGATION COMPANY ENGINE NO. 80 (8-0451-H-22) uncataloged

84 SNOWSLIDE, CANYON CREEK (8-X439a)

85 BLACK BEAR SNOWSLIDE (8-X35)

86 ROTARY SNOWPLOW AT THE WATER TANK (8-X238b)

87 ROTARY SNOWPLOW ON THE S-BRIDGE (8-X49a)

88 S-BRIDGE WRECK (8-X253)

89 NORTHERN PACIFIC DEPOT (8-B34)

91 FLOOD, WALLACE, 1906 (8-X94)

93 WALLACE AFTER THE 1890 FIRE (8-X488)

94 FIRE DEPARTMENT HORSES, WALLACE (8-X687a)

95 *(above)* WALLACE BEFORE THE 1910 FIRE (8-X504)

95 *(below)* WALLACE AFTER THE 1910 FIRE (8-X478)

97 AFTER THE FIRE, WALLACE, 1910 (8-X90)

98 OK BARBER SHOP (8-041-1)

101 SIXTH STREET, WALLACE (8-X581o)

102 BEER WAGON (8-A221)

103 WALLACE LAUNDRY (8-X287)

104 WALLACE CIGAR COMPANY (8-0539a)

105 COEUR D'ALENE IRONWORKS (8-X56)

106 PATENTED SIDE-DUMP ORE CAR, COEUR D'ALENE HARDWARE (8-X58a)

107 PUNCTURE-PROOF TIRE DEMONSTRATION (8-X651b)

108 YELLOWSTONE GARAGE (8-X791)

109 GOLDEN RULE STORE, BARNARD BLOCK (8-X409b)

110 LINEMAN (8-X10)

111 PAINTERS' UNION (8-X330)

112 COMBINATION WINDOW DISPLAY OF CANNED VEGETABLES (8-X1008)

113 WALLACE MEAT COMPANY (8-X860b)

115 JANTZEN SWIMSUIT DISPLAY, MORROW RETAIL STORE (8-X55)

116 WALLACE-BURKE GUN CLUB (8-X1018a)

119 OLD MISSION (8-X171)

120 Providence Hospital, exterior (8-B508)

121 Sunday school picnic (8-0139)

122 & 123 Kingston Boat Party, Coeur d'Alene River (8-X331)

124 Mullan school, interior (8-C-31b)

125 Wallace High School, exterior (8-A296)

126 Burke High School's girls basketball team (8-A14)

127 *(above)* Kellogg baseball team (8-0534-J) uncataloged

127 *(below)* Burke Miners' Union No. 10 tug-of-war team (8-X242)

128 Grand Theatre (8-X1003)

130 Wallace Police Department (8-A170)

133 Theodore Roosevelt in Wallace (8-X181)

134 Soldiers leaving for the Mexican expedition (8-X343)

136 American War Mothers at the Stone residence (8-0908)

137 Red Cross window (8-0543)

139 Two-man band, Montana Saloon (8-082)

141 Unidentified prostitute. *above* (23941) and *below* (23939)

142 Elks Boxing Team (8-0562c)

143 "Wallpaper Store" (8-X778)

144 Still near Silver Cliff Mine above Pottsville (8-X692)

146 Clowns with bicycles (8-0494-J) uncataloged

148 Ackerly baby with telephone (8-558)

149 Boy in overalls with ball (8-0526-J5b) uncataloged

150 Airplane patent (8-X810)

152 Mrs. Stanly A. Easton and children (8-1638)

153 Young Firpo (8-12481)

154 Patrick Murphy (8-5067)

155 Evelyn Ross Field (8-10238-3)

156 Dewey Smith (8-1175)

157 Lana Turner and mother (8-12271)

158 Idaho Mine (8-X1029b)

170 1891 map of Coeur d'Alene mining district (8-A267)

The photographs listed above are housed at the University of Idaho Library Special Collections, Moscow, Idaho. Unless otherwise indicated, they are part of the Barnard–Stockbridge Collection.

INDEX

Accident Gulch, 24
Ackerly, baby, *148*
Alexander, Moses (Governor), 132
Allison, Leon. *See* Siringo, Charles
American National Red Cross, 134, *137*
American War Mothers, *136*
Arizona Placer Mine, *23*
Armani Brothers, *142*
ASARCO (American Smelting and Refining Company), 40
Aulbach, Adam, 18, 22, 23, 57, 142
Avalanches: at Black Bear, 84, *84;* at Canyon Creek, 84, *84*

Bank of Wallace, 38
Barbershops, 100–102, *100*
Bardelli, Guido (Young Firpo, the Young Bull of Burke), *153*
Barnard, Enoch (son of Thomas Nathan), 6
Barnard, Laura Larsen (Mrs. Thomas Nathan), 3, 6, 9
Barnard, Nathan (son of Thomas Nathan), 6
Barnard, Thomas Nathan, *x, 2, 3, 4,* 10; youth of, 1–2; at Miles City, MT, 1–2, 3; and L. A. Huffman, 1–2, 3, 4; and F. J. Haynes, 4; early training, 1–2, 3, 4; in Washington Territory, 2–3; as landscape photographer, 2, 4; in the Coeur d'Alenes, 3–4; children of, 6; as mining photographer, 9; as portrait photographer, 4–6, 147; and publishing, 4, 6; at the Idaho Mine, *160;* and local politics, 6, 9; as real estate developer, 112; later career of, 6, 8–9
Barnard, William (son of Thomas Nathan), 6
Barnard Building, 8, 10, *109,* 112, 147
Barnard Studio, *11;* at the Barnard Building, 112, 147; collection, 159–161; commercial work, 9; early portraits, 10; mining photographs, 9
b'Damn, Molly, 18
Beer. *See* Breweries
Beale, Mrs. Charles W., 134
Beatty, James H. (Judge), 56
Bed Rock Flume Company, 20
Black, Clara Stockbridge (sister of Nellie Jane), 6
Black, Rev. Henry, 6
Black Bear, Idaho, 84, *84*
Blasting, 28–32
Bloom, Charlie, *144*
Boardinghouses, 45–47; Morning Mine, 46–47; profitability, 46, 47; Snowstorm, 46, *46*
Borah, William (Senator), 64, 132; in Steunenberg murder trial, 66
Boyce, Edward, 57
Bradley, Fred: manager, Bunker Hill, 38; control of Hecla, 40
Brewer, family of, 114–115

Breweries, *102,* 105–106
Bull pens: in 1892, 56; in 1899, 63–64, *63, 65,* 66, *67*
Bunker Hill and Sullivan Mine: discovery of, 36; and 1899 mining war, 57–60; and 1892 mining war, 54; and 1896 mill attack, 57; and the founding of Wardner, 74; "Glory Hole" at, *39;* mill dynamited, 58–60, *59, 60;* open cut mining at, *39;* ownership of, 36, 38; and permit system, 66; Simeon Reed and, 38; smelter, 35; and unions, 49, 50, 54
Burbridge, Frederick, 58
Burke, Idaho, 54, 71, *73, 74;* as center of union activity, 76; founding, 73–74; girls basketball team, *126;* gun club, *118;* Union No. 10 tug-of-war team, *127*
Butte and Coeur d'Alene Mine, *31*

Cages, 34; Morning Mine, *30,* 34; skips, 32
Cameras, 3; portrait, *9,* 148; stereoscopic, 2
Canyon Creek: avalanches, 84, *84;* floods, 90–92, *91*
Cardoner, Dan, 44
Carlin, William P. (Colonel), 54–55
Carter, E. D., 72
Carter Hotel, 72, 104
Cataldo, Idaho: 1892 "massacre" at, 54; and the narrow-gauge railroad, 82; as steamboat landing, 79, 82
Cataldo Mission. *See* Coeur d'Alene (Cataldo) Mission
Catholic Church: and the Coeur d'Alene Indians, 117–118; and the Coeur d'Alene Mission, 117–118, *119;* and the movies, 128; and Providence Hospital, 118–124, *120*
Century Magazine, 16
Chinese, 18, 56
Churches: picnic, *121,* 124. *See also* Catholic Church
Cigars, *104,* 106
Clement, Victor M., 38, 50
Coeur d'Alene City, Idaho, 79
Coeur d'Alene Fruit Store, *142*
Coeur d'Alene Hardware Company, *106,* 110
Coeur d'Alene Indians, 82, 117–118
Coeur d'Alene Iron Works, *105,* 106–110
Coeur d'Alene Miners' Union, 50, 118
Coeur d'Alene Mining Company, 24
Coeur d'Alene (Cataldo) Mission, 117–118, *119*
Coeur d'Alene Railway and Navigation Company, 82
Coeur d'Alene River, North Fork, gold rush to, 15–16
Coeur d'Alene River, South Fork: floods, 90–92, *91;* railroad and, 82
Coeur d'Alene Sun, 3, 18, 57, 72, 73
Combination store, *112*
Company stores, 47, 50
Compressed air, *34,* 37

Corbin, D. C., 82
Corcoran, Paul, 64
Cunningham, Richard A. (sheriff), 55
Curtis, J. F. (Colonel), 54, 56

Darrow, Clarence, 44, 66
Day, Eleanor, 102
Day, Eugene, 40, 110
Day, Harry, 134; builds mill, 35; discovers Hercules Mine, 40; and the
    Northern Pacific, 74
Day, Henry, 159, 160
DeSmet, Fr. Pierre, 117
Delta, Idaho, 24
Dodge Bros. *See* Yellowstone Garage
Double-jacking. *See* Drilling—hand
Dream Gulch, *23, 24*
Drilling: methods, 30, *31*; steel, 28, 29
—hand, 27, 28; contests, 28, *28*; double-jacking, 28, *39*; single-jacking,
    28, *28, 39*;
—machine: dry pneumatic drills, 30; jackleg, 30; Leyner, George, 30;
    wages for, 50; water hammer drills, 30, *31*
Dunlap, Rufus, *18*
Dynamite, 28–32; hazards of, 28–29, 32; as weapon, 54, 60, 66

Eagle City, Idaho, 15
Easton, Mrs. Stanly and children, *152*
Edmiston, George T. ("The King"), 68
Electricity, 34-35
Entertainment, 138; baseball, *127*, 128; basketball, *126*, 128; boxing,
    128, *142, 153*; gun club, *118*; movies, 128, *128*; picnics, *121*, 124,
    124; saloons, 138, *139*; theaters, 138; tug-of-war, *127*
Explosives. *See* Dynamite

Federal Mining and Smelting Company, 39, 40, 74
Field, Evelyn Ross, *155*
Fire: of 1890, 4, *93*; in mills, 36; of 1910, 92-97, *95, 97*; protection, 92,
    94; and Providence Hospital, 118–121
Fort Keogh, 2, 55-56
Fort Missoula, 54
Foundries, *105, 106*, 106–110
France, Dr. Hugh, 64, 67
Frank and Kramer Garage, *106*
Frisco Mine and Mill, *48, 50*, 56; dynamited, *51*; and 1892 mining
    war, *51*, 54; in 1899 mining war, 58
Fulton, Charles W., 132

Gambling, 134, 136, 138
Gases, underground: carbon dioxide, 35; carbon monoxide, 32, 35;
    carbon oxide and nitrous, 29
Gem, Idaho, 52, 54, 71, 105
Gem Mine: in 1892 mining war, 52, 54; Kneebone killed at, 57; scene of
    1893 strike, 56

Gem Miners' Union, 52, 56, 64
Gold rush, 15–16
Golden Chest mine, 23
Golden Rule Store. *See* J. C. Penney's Golden Rule Store
Goode, George, 38
Gorge Gulch, 40, *42*, 74
Grand Theatre, 128, *128*
Green, Vivian, 23
Guggenheim family, 24; smelter monopoly, 38, 40
Gun Club, Wallace-Burke, *118*

Hammond, John Hays, 38
Hanna, Marcus, 132
Harper, Fred, 40, 100
Hanson, Walter (mayor), 94
Harrison, Benjamin (President), 52, 54
Harrison, Idaho, 54
Hauser, Samuel T., 36
Haynes, Frank Jay: at Murray, Idaho, 3; and the Northern Pacific
    Railroad, 1, 2; photographic collection, 161; and western photography,
    4; and Yellowstone National Park, 2
Haywood, Bill, 66
Hecla Mine, 40, *41*
Heinz Company, *112*
Hercules Mine; *28*, 35, *36*, 40–44
Heyburn, Weldon (Senator), 131–132
Hill, James J., 88
Hillard, Barry, 24
Holohan, Peter J., 72
Homestead, Pennsylvania, 52
Horsley, Albert. *See* Orchard, Harry
Hospital, Providence, 50, 118–124, *120*
Howes and King, 104
Huffman, Laton Alton: and F. J. Haynes, 1; at Fort Keogh, 2; at Miles
    City, MT, 1-2, 3; photographic collections, 160-161; and western
    photography, 2, 4
Huffman, Perrin Cuppy (father of Laton Alton), 1
Hunt, Frank (Governor), 68
Hussey, Charles, 38
Hussey, Warren, 38
Hutton, Levi "Al", 44, 58, 62
Hutton, May Arkwright, 44, 64

Idaho militia. *See* Idaho National Guard
Idaho Mine, *160*
Idaho National Guard: in Bunker Hill mine, 56; in 1899 mining war,
    62; in 1892 mining war, 52, 54, 56; and the Mexican expedition,
    132-134, *134*; weapons stolen from, 57, 58; World War I, 134
Idaho State Tribune, 58
Industrial Workers of the World (IWW): paraphernalia, display of, *68*;
    and Western Federation of Miners, 56
Irish Fan, 76

J. C. Penney's Golden Rule Store, 110-112, *109*
J. R. Marks and Co., 72
Jantzen, promotional display, *115*
Jones, D. S. (son of), *149*

Kellogg, Noah, 36, 38
Kellogg, Idaho, 63, 82
Kelly, Fred (firechief), 94
Ketch, Fred, 128

Last Chance Mine, 77
Laundries, 102-105, *103*
Lee's puncture-proof tires, *106*
Lemeux, S. D., 74
Leyner, George, 30
Linemen, *110*
Lockman, Jacob, 105
Louisiana Purchase Exposition, *124*

Mace, Idaho, 71
McCarthy, James F., 40
McKinlay, Alexander D., 72
McKinley, William (President), 62, 66
McRae, Alexander P. (Sandy), 81, *81*
Magnuson, Richard, 159
Martial law, 55, 63
Meat, 112-115, *112*
Merriam, Henry Clay (Brigadier General), 62, 66
Mexican expedition, 132-134, *134*
Milo Gulch, 36
Mine ownership, types of: 35
Mine Owners' Protective Association (MOA), 50, 66, 160
Miners: clothing, 44; food, 45, *45,* 46; hours, 45; living conditions, 45-47; muckers, 32; nationalities of, 18, 27, 28, 44-45; wages, 44, 50, 52, 56, 57; working conditions, 44
Mining, gold, methods: dredging, 24; hydraulic, *23,* 24, *24;* placer, 19-20, *23,* 24, *24;* quartz, 20-23; water and, 19-20
Mining, hardrock, methods: blasting, 28-32; concentrating and milling, 35; drilling, 27-28, 32; mucking, 32; power, 34-35; timbering, 32-34; transport, 34
Mining, hazards of, 28-29, 32, 35, 50, 121-124
Mining equipment, local manufacture, *105,* 106-110; *106*
Mining wars, 1892, 49-56
Mining wars, 1899, 57-68
Montana Saloon, 138, *139*
Morgan, J. P., 88
Morganer, Dr., 20

Mormon Lil, 76
Morning Mine, 38-40; boardinghouse at, 46-47; Grouse Gulch Compressor, 34, *37*
Morrow Retail Store, *115, 128*
Mother Lode: "Boys" *16;* mill *21,* 23; mine, *16,* 22-23
Mowery, Charles R., 132
Moyer, Charles H., 66
Muckers. *See* Miners
Mullan, John (Lieutenant), ix
Mullan, Idaho, *28,* 71; schools, *124,* 126-128
Mullan Military Road, ix, 79
Murphy, Patrick, *154*
Murray, Idaho, 3, *16;* as center of the Coeur d'Alenes, 19; crime in, 18; decline of, 23, 24; founding of, 16; as Shoshone County seat, 19; and the Yukon Gold Company, 24
Murray Sun, 20
Murrayville. *See* Murray, Idaho

National forests (federal forest reserves), 132
Natural disasters. *See* Fires; Floods; Avalanches
Negatives, 8; Barnard-Stockbridge collection, 159-160; dry-plate, 2, 4, 10, *124;* nitrocellulose-based film, 10; wet-plate, 2
North Idaho Press, 96
North Idaho Whiskey Rebellion. *See* Prohibition
Northern Pacific Railroad: depot in Wallace of, 88-90, *89;* and the gold rush of 1883, 15; and the Hercules mine, 74; from Montana to the Coeur d'Alenes, 82-83; and the 1910 fire, 118-121; rotary snowplow, 86-88, *86, 87;* through the Tiger Hotel, 74; train stolen in 1899, 58, 60. *See also* Coeur d'Alene Railway and Navigation Company

OK Barber Shop, 100-102, *100*
Old Mission. *See* Coeur d'Alene (Cataldo) Mission
Old Wash Channel, 19, 20
Orchard, Harry, 44, 66
Ore cars, *32,* 34, *106,* 110
Oregon Railway and Navigation Company, 82; Engine No. 80, *83;* depot, *97*
Ore-or-no-go Mine. *See* Hecla Mine

Pacific Hotel, *97*
Painters' union, *111*
Paulsen, Gus, 42-44
Pelton wheel, 34, *37*
Penney, James Cash, 112
Permit system, 66-68
Pershing, John J. (General), 132-134
Pettibone, George A., 55, 66
Photographic collections: Barnard-Huffman, 160-161; Barnard-Stockbridge, 159-161; F. Jay Haynes, 161; Huffman, 161
Pierce, Idaho, 19

Pinkerton Detective Agency, 52; at Bunker Hill mine, 56. *See also* Siringo, Charles

Placer Center. *See* Wallace

Point, Fr. Nicolas, 118

Police: photographs for, 150; Wallace, *132*

Populist Party, 66; Barnard and, 6, 9, 12; in 1894 elections, 57

Potts, B. P. (Judge), 92

Prichard, A. J., 15, 16

Prichard Creek: camps on, 15-16; dredging of, 24; and gold strike, 15; hydraulicking of, 24; placer deposits on, 16, 19, 20

Prohibition, 141-144; and local breweries, *105*

Prostitution, 135-138, *141, 142,* 150; and the Barnard Studio, 10, 150, *141*

Providence Hospital, 118-124, *120*

Quigley, Dr. F. Leo, 121

Railroads: in the mines, 32; narrow-gauge, 36, 82; rates, 50, 52; survey for transcontinental, ix. *See also* under railroad name

Ravalli, Fr. Antonio, 118

Red Cross. *See* American National Red Cross

Reed, Simeon, 38

Reeves, Charles H. "Dad"; 40, 44, 100-102

Richie, W. A., 126

Rockefeller, John D., 39

Roosevelt, Theodore (President), 44, 131-132, *132*

Rossi, Bernice Johnson (Mrs. Herman J.), 140

Rossi, Herman, 92, 138-142, *142*

St. Elmo Hotel, *97*

Samuels Hotel, 140

Sanborn, I. W. (Captain), 54

Scabs. *See* Strikebreakers

Schools, 124-128; at Mullan, *124,* 126-128; at Wallace, *125,* 126

Sheeley, P. (U.P. engineer), *82*

Sherman Silver Purchase Act, 56

Sherwin, E. A., 72

Silicosis, 35

Silver, prices, 50, 56

Sims, Dr. W. S. (coroner), 55

Sinclair, Bartlett, 62, 63, 64, 66

Single-jacking. *See* Drilling—hand

Siringo, Charles, 52, 54

Sisters of Charity, 118

Smalley, Eugene, 16

Smelting, 35, 36, 38

Smith, Archie, *18*

Smith, Dewey, *156*

Smith, Sarah E. (Mrs. James R. "Hecla"), 40

Snowplows, rotary, 84-88, *86, 87;* on the Northern Pacific cutoff, 86-87, *87;* "S" bridge wreck, 86-87, *88*

Snowslides. *See* Avalanches

Snowstorm Mining Company, 46, *46*

SnyBar cabin, *16*

Spokane Falls, 34

Spokane Mining Exchange, 38

Spokane National Bank, 38

Spokesman-Review, 72, 132, 135, 138

Sports. *See* Social activities

Stages, 81-82, *81*

Steamboats, 79-80, *80*

Still, *144*

Stockbridge, Frederick A. (father of Nellie Jane), 6, 8

Stockbridge, Grace (sister of Nellie Jane), 6, *11*

Stockbridge, Nellie Jane, *6, 12,* 96; early life and training, 6-8; as businesswoman, 6, 8, 9, 10, 100; as photographer, 8, 9, 147-150; as preservationist, 10; later career of, 10-12

Stockbridge, Sarah Fenton (mother of Nellie Jane), 6, 8

Strikebreakers, 52, 56, 58

Steunenberg, Frank (Governor), 58, 60, 62, 66

Success Mine, interior, *32*

Sunset Brewery, 96, *102,* 105-106

Sweeny, Charles, 39

Taft, William Howard (President), 93

Taylor, James H., 110

Thompson Falls, Montana, 19

Tiger Hotel, 74, *74,*

Tiger-Poorman mines, 74

Timber: industry, and steamboats, 80; in mining, 32-34

Trials: after 1899 mining war, 64; after 1892 mining war, 56, 57; for Steunenberg murder, 66

Turner, Lana, *157*

Union Pacific Railroad, 82, *82. See also* Oregon Railway and Navigation Company; Washington and Idaho Railway Company

Unions: Bunker Hill and, 49, 50, 54, 56, 57; Coeur d'Alene Miners' Union, 50; 1899 mining war, 57-68; 1892 mining war, 49-56; first in Coeur d'Alenes, 49

United States Army: black troops, *52,* 62; in 1899 mining war, 62; in 1892 mining war, 54-55; encampment, *55;* 4th Infantry, 54, 55; and 1910 fire, 96; officers, *61;* 24th Infantry, 62; 22nd Infantry, *52,* 55

United States Congress: hearings on 1899 mining wars, 66

United States Supreme Court: declared permit system illegal, 67; in 1892 mining wars, 56

University of Idaho, 159

University of Idaho Library, 159-160

Villa, Pancho, 132

Volstead Act. *See* Prohibition

Wallace, Colonel William R., 71–73; and claim dispute, 72–73; Ore-or-no-go ownership, 40

Wallace, Lucy (Mrs. W. R.), 72

Wallace, Idaho, 71–72, *72, 95;* and claim dispute, 72–73; fire of 1890, 4, *93,* fire of 1910, 90–96, *95, 97;* flood of 1906, 90–92, *91;* local business, 99–115; narrow-gauge railroad to, 72; schools, 124–126, *125;* Sixth Street, *101*

Wallace Cigar Company, *104,* 106

Wallace Free Press, 72

Wallace Laundry, *103,* 104–105

Wallace Meat Company, 112–115, *112*

Wallace Press-Times, 110, 138

Wallace Times: and the fire of 1910, 94

Wardner, Jim, 36

Wardner, Idaho, 28, 71, 76, *76, 77;* founding, 73–74; and the Bunker Hill, 74, 76

Wardner Junction. *See* Kellogg, Idaho

Washington and Idaho Railway Company, 82

Water rights, 36

Weniger, R. E. (sheriff), 142, *144*

Western Federation of Miners (WFM), 56–57; permit system and, 67; and Steunenberg murder, 60, 66

White and Bender, *91,* 104

Willey, Norman B. (Governor), 54, 55

Wilson, Woodrow (President), 132, 134

Woods, W. W. (Judge), 136, 140

World War I, 134

Yellowstone Garage, *108*

Young, James D. (sheriff), 58, 64

Yukon Gold Company, 24

Zinc, 35

Library of Congress Cataloging in Publication Data

Hart, Patricia, 1950-
  Mining Town.

  1. Miners—Coeur d'Alene Mountains (Idaho and Mont.)—History—
  Pictorial works. 2. Miners—Idaho—Wallace in History—Pictorial
  works. 3. Barnard, T. N. (Thomas Nathan)—Photograph collections.
  4. Stockbridge, Nellie—Photograph collections. I. Nelson, Ivar. II.
  Title.

HD8039.M61U47

1984

779'9979691

84—40325

ISBN: 0-295-96105-8

MINING TOWN

Designed by Dana Sloan
Composed by North Country Book Express
in Compugraphic Baskerville with display lines
in Windsor Light Condensed
Printed by Kingsport Press
on Lustro Offset Dull Enamel
Bound by Kingsport Press
in Devon Gray and
stamped in gunmetal

Produced at North Country Book Express
by Connie Bollinger, Karen Cathcart,
and Mary Schierman